"As a former phobic, I appreciate Carol's sensiti~~v~~ ~~approach to the~~ scary issues of life. This isn't a book—it's a healing balm!"

—Patsy Clairmont, author of *Normal Is Just a Setting on Your Dryer* and *God Uses Cracked Pots*

"For women who have locked their fears in the closet and now are afraid to leave the house unguarded, this book offers clarification, fellowship, and hope for healing."

—Jeannette Clift George, coauthor of *Travel Tips from a Reluctant Traveler*

"Here is a must-read book for all women who ask, 'Where's the joy in life?' With sensitivity and wisdom, Carol Kent helps women identify and face one of the deadliest enemies of the human spirit—fear."

—Jan Stoop, coauthor of *Saying Goodbye to Disappointments*

TAME YOUR FEARS

AND TRANSFORM THEM *into*
FAITH, CONFIDENCE, AND ACTION

CAROL KENT

NAVPRESS

Bringing Truth to Life
P.O. Box 35001, Colorado Springs, Colorado 80935

OUR GUARANTEE TO YOU

We believe so strongly in the message of our books that
we are making this quality guarantee to you. If for any
reason you are disappointed with the content of this
book, return the title page to us with your name and
address and we will refund to you the list price of the
book. To help us serve you better, please briefly describe
why you were disappointed. Mail your refund request to:
NavPress, P.O. Box 35002, Colorado Springs, CO 80935.

The Navigators is an international Christian organization. Our mission is to reach, disciple, and equip people to
know Christ and to make Him known through successive generations. We envision multitudes of diverse people
in the United States and every other nation who have a passionate love for Christ, live a lifestyle of sharing
Christ's love, and multiply spiritual laborers among those without Christ.

NavPress is the publishing ministry of The Navigators. NavPress publications help believers learn biblical truth
and apply what they learn to their lives and ministries. Our mission is to stimulate spiritual formation among our
readers.

Cover design by David Carlson Design
Cover illustration by Kathleen Finlay/Masterfile
Creative Team: Nanci McAlister, Karen Lee-Thorp, Darla Hightower, Pat Miller

Some of the anecdotal illustrations in this book are true to life and are included with the permission of the per-
sons involved. All other illustrations are composites of real situations, and any resemblance to people living or
dead is coincidental.

Unless otherwise identified, all Scripture quotations in this publication are taken from the *THE MESSAGE* (msg).
Copyright © 1993, 1994, 1995, 1996, 2000, 2001, 2002. Used by permission of NavPress Publishing Group.
Other versions used include: *HOLY BIBLE: NEW INTERNATIONAL VERSION®* (niv). Copyright © 1973, 1978,
1984 by International Bible Society. Used by permission of Zondervan Publishing House. All rights reserved; the
New King James Version (nkjv), copyright ©1979, 1980, 1982, 1990, Thomas Nelson Inc., Publishers; *The Living
Bible* (tlb),copyright © 1971, used by permission of Tyndale House Publishers, Inc., Wheaton, IL 60189, all
rights reserved; and the *King James Version* (kjv).

Kent, Carol, 1947-
  Tame your fears : and transform them into faith, confidence, and
action / Carol Kent.
      p. cm.
Includes bibliographical references.
  ISBN 1-57683-359-3
  1. Christian women--Religious life. 2. Fear--Religious
aspects--Christianity. I. Title.
  BV4527 .K453 2003
  248.8'43--dc21

                                    2002015679

Printed in the United States of America

1 2 3 4 5 6 7 8 9 / 07 06 05 04 03

FOR A FREE CATALOG OF
NAVPRESS BOOKS & BIBLE STUDIES,
CALL 1-800-366-7788 (USA)
or 1-416-499-4615 (CANADA)

CONTENTS

This book is lovingly dedicated to my son
Jason Paul Kent

ACKNOWLEDGMENTS

Some authors are "writers who occasionally speak." I am a speaker who occasionally writes. In practical terms, that means the time it takes to write a book is not scheduled on my daily calendar. Several support people have come alongside at precisely the right moments to enable me to roll a manuscript off the computer (almost) on time and turn in a finished project. I am indebted to these incredible people: My editor, Traci Mullins—I am convinced that a mediocre editor explains; a good editor guides; a superior editor encourages during the process of explaining and guiding; and a great editor inspires and confronts, while giving confidence to an author. Traci is a rare gem as an editor. Her creative genius is woven throughout this project and her ability to combine professionalism and friendship made the writing process a pleasure!

My husband, Gene Kent—This man lives out the true meaning of what Christian marriage is supposed to be. He envelops me with respect, humor, friendship, and passion. He frees me to meet deadlines without guilt and brings me chocolate candy bars when I'm brain dead.

My sisters—Jennie Dimkoff, Paula Afman, Bonnie Emmorey, and Joy Carlson—I never get tired of the question, "Are all of those girls really in your family?" Growing up with so many women was a wonderful experience. Each of my sisters has overcome paralyzing fear to become the woman of influence she is today. Thanks to each of you for loving me intensely and for encouraging me along the way.

My administrative assistant, Shelly Aldrich—One day I took a step of faith and hired this woman to answer correspondence, handle phone calls, order office supplies, deal with interruptions, run errands, and feed my cat in my absence. (What a job description!) She makes me look better than I deserve and has freed me to do what God called me to do without getting trapped in paperwork.

My friends and prayer supporters—I am indebted to Sherrie Eldridge, Janet Fleck, Rhua Bliss, and Anne Denmark for sharing their personal journeys as illustrations in this book; Ginger Sisson, Deborah K. Jones, Kathe Wunnenberg, and Barbara Owlsley spent hours researching the topic of fear and provided me with countless numbers of computer printouts and copies of articles and illustrations that were invaluable during the writing process; Tommy Olmstead sent side-splitting cards filled with tasteless, hilarious humor to keep me encouraged; Linda Neff sent inspiring quotations to keep me motivated; Mama Afman prayed without ceasing, along with so many of those already listed above.

This book is a tribute to the combined efforts of each of you!

PART ONE

HOPE...
WHEN LIFE
GETS SCARY

"IF I'M SUCH A GREAT CHRISTIAN, WHY DO I HAVE THIS PROBLEM?"

Discovering We Are Not Alone

/З

Have you ever thought how infectious fear can be? It spreads from one person to another more quickly and certainly than any of the fevers we know so well.

AMY CARMICHAEL
You Are My Hiding Place

"I can't do this! I don't want to do this! I don't want to be here! I think it is totally irrational to spend all this money to terrorize myself and risk possible injury that could keep me from functioning properly for weeks to come!" My words tumbled out frantically, mingled with stifled sobs.

My husband worked quietly, but steadily, as he continued to tighten my rented ski boots in preparation for what I knew was the inevitable experience just ahead. Then, with uncharacteristic candor, he looked me in the eyes and said, "You're afraid. So what? What's the worst thing that could happen? You might fall down and you'd have to get up again."

Now I was angry. He didn't understand. Fear was a subject I knew too well. A virus I had transferred to others. A paralyzing emotion I sometimes denied but always had to face. *Why couldn't he understand the depth of my fear?*

We had lived in Michigan for years, within easy driving distance of numerous ski resorts. Every winter it always turned cold and snowy . . . and every winter I went into hibernation until the first breath of spring.

Skiing was for people who lived "on the edge," I convinced myself. It was a sport for people who did not value straight noses and unbroken bones. It was for those who thrived on adrenaline for stimulation—instead of honest work in a legitimate vocation.

But our teenage son had requested downhill skis for Christmas, and we decided to treat him to a New Year's weekend at Shanty Creek Ski Lodge. From the moment he took his first trip down the hill, he was hooked. By the second day his skis were gliding down Schuss Mountain with precise accuracy, and it was hard to get him to take breaks for meals. He had discovered *his* sport!

Halfway through the weekend my husband, Gene, said, "Honey, Jason loves skiing. He's our only child. He will probably marry a woman who likes this sport. We may spend many future vacation weekends in ski lodges. If you want to spend time with your family, you have a choice: You can sit in the lodge drinking hot chocolate by the fire for the rest of your life, or you can conquer this phobia."

He was right. I hate it when he's right, especially when I have to admit it. Besides, I had already gained my seven extra Christmas pounds, and the prospects of that hot chocolate increasing the diameter of my thighs while *they* were getting exercise did not create a desirable image. I reluctantly yielded to his suggestion and registered for a ski lesson.

Gene finished tightening my boots, then he carefully helped me balance as I moved in the direction of the bunny hill. I found myself wondering how many people had died on that hill—or worse yet, how many were permanently maimed?

He softened a bit. "Carol, I heard a speaker recently who said, 'There are only two fears we are born with: *falling* and *loud noises*. All the rest are learned or acquired.' I know you can conquer this fear!"

⊮ THE PROBLEM DEFINED

I was afraid of falling, all right. But my fear went deeper than that. His words reverberated in my mind: "all the rest are *learned* or *acquired*." Where did fear come from? How did it get so powerful? Why did it immobilize so many people? What was the origin of this monster anyway? And most of all, why did it continue to plague *me*? After all, I had been a Christian for many years. I was a leader. A speaker. An author. A wife. A mom. An educated, hardworking woman who believed the Bible and loved God. *Why did I still have this problem?*

Fear is one of our oldest and deadliest enemies. It causes illness, stifles creativity, prevents love, destroys families, depletes energy, feeds addictions, and holds people in bondage. For many women, fear is an unwanted, constant companion. In the middle of watching the destructive force of fear, sometimes we forget there's a positive side to fear as well.

Webster tells us fear is any one of several responses: "(1) anxiety and agitation caused by the presence of danger, evil, or pain; dread, fright; (2) awe, reverence; (3) a feeling of uneasiness, anxiety, concern."[1]

That definition is helpful, but even more insight comes when we investigate fear as a verb: "(1) to be afraid of, to dread" (I can identify with that!); "(2) to feel reverence or awe for" (I certainly *fear* God in that way!); "(3) to expect with misgiving . . . to *feel* fear . . . to be uneasy or anxious."[2] (*Now that's a definition I can relate to.*) And that's what this book is all about!

⅓ UNDERSTANDING THE UNDERLYING TYPES OF FEAR

There are basically three types of fear: "holy" fear, "self-preserving" fear, and "slavish" fear. The first comes from our reverence for and awe of the God who created us and loves us. The second has everything to do with the God-given instinct to run from danger, avert an accident, or protect ourselves and those we love. This "wise" form of fear causes us to take responsibility for ourselves and others. It motivates us to teach our children to look both ways before crossing the street and to use caution on a bicycle.

This book, however, is about "slavish" fear—the negative type that kills expressions of love, plugs lines of communication, imprisons victims of abuse, taunts with ridiculous phobias, controls by manipulation, and erodes all confidence and security. *Wise, self-preserving fear shifts into slavish fear when it becomes obsessive and controlling.* When a child reaches an age of maturity, and a parent prevents the development of natural independence by immobilizing him or her with fears that are not based on reality, slavish fear takes over. When a sport as regulated and exhilarating as downhill snow skiing paralyzes me because of a twenty-year-old memory of one bad experience, I am allowing myself to be victimized by fear.

Boiled down to the bottom line, the negative aspect of fear is a problem of (1) *focus* and (2) *self-reliance.* It all began in the Garden of Eden. Adam and Eve had known a perfect relationship with God. They knew Him as their creator, companion, teacher, and friend. At that time in history the only fear present was absolutely holy. There was purity in God's relationship with Adam and Eve.

After Adam and Eve disobeyed God, a change occurred. With no instruction, Adam had an instant awareness of slavish fear. When God called, Adam responded, "I heard you in the garden, and I was afraid because I was naked; so I hid" (Genesis 3:10, NIV). Instead of rushing to be with his best friend, Adam was now doubting his position, fearful of not being accepted, and hiding in the bushes.

The false roots of Adam's fear are still with us today. God had always been there for him, but self-reliance kept him from asking for help:

- Adam feared abandonment, yet he chose to abandon the One he needed the most.
- He was ashamed of revealing who he really was, yet needed to be honest with God to learn how to live in a sinful world.
- He made himself lonely because he feared rejection.
- He gave in to temptation and felt unforgiven and afraid.

When sin entered the human race, Adam's *focus* was taken off God. *Self-reliance* (and let's add *self-preservation*) kicked in, and Adam was running and hiding. (Okay. I admit it. Eve had the problem too.) And today we're still doing the same thing—running and hiding! Adam's response is a lot like mine.

Slavish fear is a natural consequence of self-reliance. Sometimes "helping myself out and doing my best in the middle of my fears" keeps me from admitting that *sin* and *self-reliance* are the same thing. Trusting in "self" as Adam did leads to shame, slavery, obsessive, controlling behavior, and thick walls of self-protection. It becomes a learned cycle that is hard to break.

Running. Hiding. Protecting myself. As Proverbs tells us, "The wicked are edgy with guilt, ready to run off even when no one's after them; Honest people are relaxed and confident, bold as lions" (28:1). All this sometimes seems complicated to me, because when I'm afraid and choosing "run and hide" behavior, I'm usually not telling myself, "Well, I'm emotionally running away from God right now, so that's why I'm feeling this overwhelming terror. It's just a problem of focus and self-reliance that I learned from Adam and Eve. I'll just change my direction."

When God asked Adam whether or not he had eaten from the forbidden tree, Adam immediately began to hurl blame in Eve's direction—a tactic I often use myself! When I'm afraid, I want to blame someone else for the problem. "The man said, 'The Woman you gave me as a companion, she gave me fruit from the tree, and, yes, I ate it'" (Genesis 3:12). When we are afraid and looking for someone to blame, our self-preservation kicks in, and we often hurl it (as Adam did) in a variety of ways.

Fear is complicated. Like Adam and Eve, sometimes we hurl blame and other times we emotionally run from God by conveniently "forgetting" past abuse that so deeply needs His healing. Or we lose ourselves in perfectionism. Perhaps we form codependent relationships with friends or relatives. Our running keeps us from revealing our doubts about God's love . . . or at times, the very *existence* of God. We dismiss prison-like phobias as "little hang-ups." We rarely reveal the true magnitude of our fear to other human beings. They might think we are weak.

Most of us have never thought much about where our fear came from or how it developed. What we *do* know is that it's a monster we live with, an emotion that's sometimes out of control. Our fear is an undesired and uninvited guest that invades the inner sanctums of our lives and establishes residency.

When fear invades, it comes with a customized wardrobe of disguises. So, for many of us, *recognizing* fear in its many forms is a lifetime struggle. *Dealing* with that fear once we've recognized it is a much greater challenge.

Fear is subtle and has many hidden forms. Attractive forms. Productive aspects. Admirable faces. Like someone dressing up for a costume party, fear can appear glamorous; the outside looks flawless, but the inside is rotting. Hurting. Hidden. Sick. Running. Dishonest. The person is masquerading as "healthy," but beneath her facade she is terminally ill.

If you picked up this book because the title caught your eye, that person might be you. Or it could be your friend, your sister, your mother, your neighbor, or your coworker. One thing you can't escape: You *do* know this person. And therefore you are responsible to do *something*. But what?

A POSITIVE SIDE TO FEAR?

Until recently, I never saw any personal benefits connected to fear. The disadvantages always seemed so obvious. I know women who are trapped in a web of spine-weakening and spirit-breaking fears. At times, I am one of those women. Some of the negative conditions fear produces are apprehension, anxiety, low productivity, loss of vitality and serenity, intimidation, paralysis, resentment, rage, and obsessive self-protection.

The plus side of all of this is that there are positive conditions fear can lead us to: awe, adrenaline, humility, a shift of focus from finite to infinite power. When I give myself permission to see the positive aspects of fear, I get a totally new focus on the potential of this powerful emotion. Fear is often viewed as a roadblock to happiness, an insurmountable obstacle on the road to success and fulfillment. In this book we will learn techniques for taming fear, for turning it into appropriate power, positive action, and love.

Peter McWilliams' words remind us of the benefit of fear: "Fear provides the energy to do your best in a new situation. When you're afraid, your senses sharpen, your eyes narrow, you have more adrenaline, more precise focus, more energy. You are more aware."[3]

FIVE FORMS OF FEAR

Before we talk about the solution, we need to identify slavish fear in its many forms. I have asked women all over the United States and Canada what their fears are. Their answers have convinced me that geographical location, economic background, educational credentials, denominational affiliation, and strength of personality make little difference in the intensity of fear.

All of us have experienced the paralyzing grip of this emotion we would rather live without! The comforting factor I've discovered is that we are not alone. Here are the categories of fear that women have described to me repeatedly.

THE FEAR OF THINGS THAT HAVEN'T HAPPENED ... YET!

Fear 1: Paralyzing Phobias

Cheryl was a basket case. She was afraid of everything. If someone shook her hand, she knew she'd get a disease. If we were in a crowded room, she couldn't breathe. If we were at the beach, she didn't swim. She had phobias to go along with situations most people never dreamed could happen. Irrational panic was her constant companion—and Cheryl seemed to need a baby-sitter more than a friend.

Fear 2: Potential Disasters

Diana's husband was an hour late for dinner. With every passing minute her anxiety increased. There had been layoffs at his plant. At first factory positions were cut, and now the management team was being streamlined. A meeting was set up for that afternoon and more cuts would be discussed. What if he lost his job? How could they pay the mortgage payment? And what about the children's college tuition? What would they do? As the clock continued to mark the passing of time, she was *sure* he had received a pink slip. Her head pounded. Much of Diana's life was consumed with what she knew were "legitimate" fears of negative things that might happen to someone in her family.

THE FEAR OF BEING VULNERABLE

Fear 3: Losing Control

Kathy was greatly respected. She was the hardest-working committee member on the retreat staff. When she accepted a job, it was done correctly and quickly. Her motto seemed to be, "If it's worth doing, it's worth doing right!" Her house was immaculate. Her children were clean and well-behaved.

It was hard to get close to Kathy, because you always felt as if you were interrupting her well-planned life and her carefully scheduled day. Although her outside image was enviable, Kathy was miserable. Her family was miserable. Kathy's controlling personality and manipulation of family members were making life inside the "white picket fence" unbearable. Kathy was afraid of being vulnerable and sought to mask her fears in a prison of her own making. Her fear of losing control made everyone around her feel as if they were behind bars too!

Fear 4: Revealing Who I Really Am

Cindy was embarrassed by her background. Her father was an alcoholic, and her mother raised four children on welfare and part-time work. Cindy's greatest desire was to get an education and lift herself out of that lifestyle. A school counselor took interest in Cindy and helped her get a scholarship to an accredited university.

Life changed drastically for the young woman who had experienced poverty and the inner city. She married a dynamic, compassionate man who loved her without reservation. But Cindy was filled with fear at her husband's family reunions. Anxiety plagued her when she faced his business dinners or had to make small talk with her middle-class neighbors. Cindy's fear of self-disclosure and her shame regarding her background kept her caught in a web of insecurity.

THE FEAR OF ABANDONMENT

Fear 5: Disappointing People

"Where are you?" The voice on the cell phone was rough. Domineering. Authoritative. Parental. Kay's husband was checking up on her again. "I'm home from work early. I'm hungry and I want dinner on the table *now*! I told you it was okay for you to work as long as you took care of your responsibilities in this house first! If you're too busy to pay attention to the most important person in your life, I'll find someone who can!" He hung up.

Kay was miserably unhappy. When Steve was successful in business and able to finance his personal pleasures, he was fun to be with. When he was drinking and/or feeling financial strain, he was abusive, controlling, and obnoxious. Kay was dependent on Steve for a roof over her head, support for their son, and for proving to her parents that she had made the right choice in a husband they had questions about. She was afraid he might leave her penniless and homeless, but she was more afraid of disappointing and alienating her strict Christian mother and father, who did not approve of divorce under *any* circumstances.

Fear 6: Being Rejected

Joanne pulled the blankets up over her head. She was discouraged, depressed, and afraid. A few months ago she and her husband had a major communication breakdown. But they were Christians, so she thought they would work out their problems.

But last night he had dispassionately told her he had filed for divorce — "irreconcilable differences," the paper stated. His unemotional approach to ending the marriage was incomprehensible. They had *three* children. She was being rejected by the man she always thought loved her. What if her children chose *his* side in the divorce? What if the people at church blamed *her* for not being a better wife? What if she was alone for the rest of her life?

The sobering fear of abandonment obliterated her ability to function normally. This was unfair—cruel and unusual punishment for a woman who had devoted her whole adult life to being a good wife and mother.

THE FEAR OF TRUTH

Fear 7: Facing My Past

The letter came from an old friend. Victoria is the kind of person I always wanted to be like—immensely talented, attractive, vivacious. But beneath her energy was a deep sadness. For as long as I had known her, I sensed something was haunting her. But what?

I read, "Sometime I would like to talk with you about what I've been learning in counseling. I am in awe of what our minds are able to do—what our emotions remember but our minds forget—and I'm in greater awe of how God protects us but is still ready to help us by revealing our pain.

"I have wondered why I *couldn't* have the joy that sometimes sounds rather easy to get. . . . I'm on the verge of remembering (and exposing) some frightening things. Until that happens I can't put a lot of relationships in my life in proper perspective."

My heart is heavy for Victoria. She is afraid to face the past, but she knows there is no other way to get on with the future.

Fear 8: Losing My Faith

Joyce waited until I was alone. We were in an exquisite retreat setting in the mountains with a large group of women from her dynamic, young church. I had spotted her in the background waiting to talk to me. When the time came, her eyes flooded with tears and she strained to get the words out.

"Carol, I have no one to talk to. All these women think I'm one of their leaders, but I'm not sure I even believe in God anymore. My doubts make me ashamed. But I'm so afraid I have lost my faith completely. *Who* is God? *Where* is He? My mother just died of cancer, and my dad has heart problems. My prayers have gone unanswered. *Why* does He let innocent people suffer? I know I'm not supposed to question Him, but I don't believe anymore. How can I be a Christian and feel this way?"

Many women share this fear of losing their faith. They have nagging doubts and disbeliefs when they feel a real Christian should be able to resolve all of this.

THE FEAR OF MAKING WRONG CHOICES

Fear 9: Getting Trapped

Heather was a go-getter. She had married her high-school sweetheart at eighteen. She gave birth to two children before her twenty-second birthday. Now she was in her early thirties and feeling sad that she hadn't waited for marriage and children until after her education was completed. Her husband, Rod, was a nice guy and a good provider, but after working long hours in a local factory, he wasn't too enthusiastic about meeting her emotional or intellectual needs. Heather wanted to pursue a college degree, and Rod was feeling threatened.

Emotion enveloped Heather as she came to grips with her worst fear: being trapped in a dead-end situation. She felt that she would never be able to live up to her potential because of lost opportunity. How could she stay married to a man who held her in intellectual slavery by his own fears that she might "outgrow" him and find companionship with a more educated and refined partner?

Fear 10: Achieving Success/Admitting Failure

Carrie *loved* to write. She had kept her thoughts recorded in a journal since junior high. Carrie always knew her life would revolve around the publishing world. She obtained a degree in journalism and accepted a position as an editor with a major book publisher. Her editing skills were excellent, and she enjoyed working with the authors.

When a position opened as acquisitions editor for her publisher, she accepted the job with a sense of controlled exhilaration—and very real fear. What if she failed? What if her ideas weren't creative enough to inspire the authors she worked with? What if she pushed a project through that the rest of the editorial staff had questions about and it bombed? It would be her fault! The fear of risking her professional reputation kept her from pursuing exciting projects.

The idea of succeeding was just as threatening to Carrie. If the authors she recommended did well, that might mean an increased workload and higher expectations. Doing well could be more stressful than failing.

What Do I Do Next?

Identifying our fears and admitting we have a problem is only the beginning. Most of us have struggled for a lifetime with fear at some level. I've been frustrated by an underlying belief that "godly Christian women" aren't supposed to struggle with phobias, fears, and anxieties, because "trusting the Lord" should be more than enough to handle any problem. So I'm a failure. Now what?

The first step to finding a solution is to acknowledge that there are times when we question our faith and struggle with fear. Some of us have had fleeting thoughts of suicide. Most often, instead of physical suicide, we experience emotional suicide. Fear becomes "comfortable" because it's familiar. We're used to feeling like powerless victims in the fear monster's kingdom. Instead of taming the monster and enjoying our lives, we allow ourselves to die slowly by many of the following prescriptions: denial, addictions, withdrawal, control, shame, and self-hatred. Why?

The next chapter will take us a step further by explaining the chain reaction we go through when fear is developed and ultimately defeated. There is a way to face this monster squarely, and God has empowered us to overcome it and get on with productive and happy lives. But He never forces this on us. He lets us choose.

⅓ AN INVITATION

If you have ever asked yourself the following questions, the rest of this book was written for you:

- Are my fears the same as fears faced by other women?
- What is fear, and can it be controlled?
- Is my perfectionism actually based in the fear of being vulnerable?
- If I reveal myself to you, will you accept me—or judge me?
- Why am I afraid that the worst-case scenario will happen to me or my family?
- Why am I so afraid of being rejected, abandoned, or lonely?
- If I face the fears of the past and admit the truth, will I cause myself more pain?
- Can I really be a Christian if I struggle with fear?
- Is there a positive side to fear that could actually be a springboard to success and happiness?

Overcoming lifelong fear is inconvenient. The process destroys carefully constructed facades. It leaves one feeling naked. Unprotected. Vulnerable. Exposed. It seems odd to speak of fear as "safe," but as with any long-term companion—even a cruel one—saying goodbye is difficult. Henri Nouwen confirms the frightening risk involved in the process:

> We are afraid that the God who says He loves us will prove in the
> end to be more demanding than loving. I am convinced that the
> real reason we pray so little is fear: fear of facing God, fear also of
> facing our own and others' brokenness. I think our fearful hearts
> are saying: "Can I really trust God?"4

Facing our fear head-on can feel intensely risky. But it can be a stepping stone to humble faith, renewed confidence, appropriate power and courage, and trusting reverence toward a sovereign, powerful, and loving God. "Perfect love casts out fear."[5] It's in the Bible. And it's true. But how does it work? If you are among the few who dare to embrace change, read on.

"WHAT HAPPENS INSIDE MY HEAD WHEN I'M AFRAID?"

Recognizing and Taming Your Fears

Fear was designed by God to give our bodies the sudden bursts of strength and speed we need in emergencies. But when fear becomes a permanent condition, it can paralyze the spirit, keeping us from taking the risks of generosity, love, and vulnerability that characterize citizens of God's kingdom.

DAVID NEFF
"Christians Who Fear Too Much," Christianity Today

The long-awaited package was in the mailbox. The professional label with the return address and logo of the company confirmed my suspicions. With hands trembling, I opened the padded envelope and removed the cassette tapes. A decision had to be made. I could listen to them now or prolong the torture.

The call had come a year earlier from a woman asking if I would be willing to speak for their denominational conference. The location sounded exotic to this mother of a preschooler, who rarely got out of town, much less out of state, with private accommodations in a top-of-the-line hotel. Before the woman hung up, she asked if the group could have my presentations professionally recorded so conference participants could purchase tapes of the sessions.

I was *excited!* This was the most important opportunity in ministry that had ever come my way. A stimulating challenge! However, as the date approached, *living through* my commitment was much more taxing than I had anticipated. The preparation for the messages wasn't the problem. I had taught Bible studies for years . . . but being "good enough" for this sophisticated audience was so intimidating I wanted to back out. But it was too late.

I boarded an airplane and flew to meet this sizable group. It was the first time an organization had paid for expensive travel arrangements so that I could be their keynote speaker. Panic gripped my heart as I approached the lectern. Thoughts raced.

How could I ever be professional enough to be worth the amount of money they paid to bring me here?

What if my mouth gets so dry I am not able to speak a word? Worse yet, what if my brain leaves my body when I stand in front of the audience?

I am scared to death! What if my heart quits pumping and I die?

What if I do such a terrible job that these people tell other groups what a failure I am? (Well, at least I'd *never* have to speak in public again!)

Three weeks after the event, I realized I *did* live through the experience, and now the suspense was killing me. Did I sound as bad as I knew I was? Or by some miracle had God transformed my frayed nerves into supernatural energy? I could bear the uncertainty no longer.

I slipped the tape into the cassette player and pushed "PLAY." The magnetic tape rolled, but the inferior quality of the recording surprised me. With my opening remarks came a loud, unnerving "thump, thump, thump" that reverberated over the recorded message. It was so unrelenting and distracting it was hard to follow the central idea. Then, as the minutes rolled on, there was more airtime between thumps, and finally, ten minutes into the talk, all discernable thumping stopped. What was the problem? A reputable company had done the recording. As I pondered the confusing situation, a piece of paper fluttered to the floor from the padded envelope. It read:

> Dear Mrs. Kent,
>
> When we heard the recording of your first talk, we thought our equipment was terribly defective. But the longer we listened, we realized our sensitive microphone was just picking up the sound of your beating heart. Obviously, you relaxed after awhile!

⁄₃ DISSECTING THE REAL PROBLEM

Fear has so many forms that sometimes a solution seems elusive. On numerous occasions I have tried to "talk myself out of" fearful feelings. It never worked, although it did make me feel like I was doing something. Whether the problem is as basic as the fear of public speaking or as psychologically deep as the fear of abandonment or betrayal, some basic definitions can help us to form a framework for dealing with the problem.

The solution to overcoming fear is not positive self-talk or a greater effort to control my own behavior or the behavior of others. *The solution is a broken humility and trust in a sovereign, engaged, and loving God.*

But how does that work? What sounds logical, or even like "the proper spiritual response," on paper is often much more difficult to experience in real-life situations.

My friend Nancy has a distorted concept of God because her father abused her. If the solution to the fear problem is to let God be the ultimate deliverer and protector, how can she address her fear or rage toward God for apparently abandoning her in the past? Her fears are great. Her rage seems justified. God seems far away and uninvolved in her life—and cruel. Why would a loving God have allowed the abuse to take place? Most days it's easier for her to disguise her problem than to identify her basic fears and deal with them.

We might like to think that only those who have been emotionally devastated struggle with fear, but that's not always true. Paul Moede sheds light on this:

> Fear is not the private domain of the weak. It strikes at the best
> of us. It does not restrict itself to the individual but, like a virus,
> it can be transmitted to others. And its most dangerous aspect—
> especially for the Christian—is its ability to slap handcuffs and
> shackles on life, to keep the believer who wears them bound up
> in a prison of frustration and hopelessness.[1]

How do we get so distorted in our thinking—so brainwashed by the fear monster? We need to take a closer look at those sneaky little human propensities mentioned earlier.

13 TERROR AT SEA

The setting is the Sea of Galilee.[2] Jesus Christ's public ministry is in its heyday. People have been healed. Demon-possessed men have been delivered. Thousands have been fed with a little boy's lunch. Pretty newsworthy stuff!

Jesus is physically exhausted. Emotionally spent. In need of time with His Father. The disciples get into the boat and go ahead of Him. He dismisses the crowd and goes into the hills for a time of prayer. As evening comes, a storm threatens. The boat is thrashed around by rowdy waves.

The wind grows harsh. Jesus walks on the water toward His friends.

The scared-stiff disciples think He's a ghost and scream in terror. Jesus *immediately* responds, "Take courage! It is I. Don't be afraid." Impulsive Peter gets inspired and wants to walk on the water to meet Him. He gets out of the boat, heads in Jesus' direction, recognizes the destructive force of the wind, and panics!

He screams, "Lord, save me!" *Immediately* Jesus reaches out to him, saves him from his worst fear, comforts him, and builds a spiritual lesson out of the event.

Peter had the same problem we have: *focus* and *self-reliance.* The story is easier to understand when we see ourselves on the page.

1. *Uncertain circumstances*—Almost every time I deal with fear, I face uncertain circumstances—just like the disciples did. My situation seems unfamiliar. My boat is rocking. My favorite Captain does not seem to be on board. My future is unknown.

2. *Wrong conclusions*—In the middle of my panic, I often look at the obvious instead of the supernatural. Instead of seeing Jesus supernaturally at work in the middle of my storm, I see all kinds of ghosts, represented by my personal fears. Sometimes I voice my fears loudly as the disciples did. Other times I feel angry and powerless. "Where is Jesus when I need Him most?"

3. *Impulsive conduct*—Peter's "jump-out-of-the-boat" behavior reminds me of myself. Sometimes I cry, "Lord, if You are *really* here, in the middle of my panic and my frightening situation, prove Yourself supernaturally. I mean, *do* something so I know it's You!"

4. *Desperate call*—When I, like Peter, step out in trust, I sometimes take my eyes off Him and focus on my terrorizing circumstances. The "winds of fear" look much worse than they did before I tried to trust Him. I cry, "Lord, save me!"

5. *Immediate calm*—Without delay He reaches out to me and says, "You of little faith . . . why did you doubt?" And in the security of His

compassionate eye contact and warm, affirming grip, my heart begins the measured, careful journey toward accepting His perfect love. There it is—spelled out in the Bible. Jesus is the solution to the terrors around us. So why do so many of us not experience this immediate calming connection with God in the middle of our overwhelming fears? What can we do when Jesus doesn't "fix" our situation? This book will address those questions.

SIX DISGUISES OF FEAR

Many of us have lived behind our disguises for so long we hardly recognize that fear motivates many of our destructive behaviors. I have, at times, starred in all the roles in the play "The Six Disguises of Fear." Sometimes my performances have been worthy of standing ovations. One role could have brought me an Oscar. The beginning of positive change comes when we leave our costumes in the dressing room after admitting to one of the following roles:

1. A *perfectionist* lifestyle: "If I can please all of the people in my life with flawless behavior and control everything and everyone around me, I won't have to admit my deep insecurities and fears."

2. A *possessive* nature: "If I can protect the people I love the most by establishing the borders of their activities and guarding the dimensions of their interactions with other people, I will safeguard them from fearful experiences."

3. A *"picky"* attitude: "If I can criticize someone else, I will look better. I won't have to admit that it makes me feel like a bigger and less fearful person when I put somebody else's personality or methods down in order to secure my own position."

4. A *pretentious* faith: "If I make a list of what *real* Christians do and don't do and show people my saintliness in action, perhaps I can cover up

my fears, which are usually expressed through pride, inflexibility, legalism, and condemnation of 'less godly' people."

5. A *passionate* workaholism: "If I invest my total energy in worthy causes and/or work hard enough to earn the approval of my superiors, I'll be too tired to worry about my fears. If I just keep busy enough with my family responsibilities and personal activities, I won't have to acknowledge the ache inside of me and admit that I don't know how to give or receive love."

6. A *plastic* smile: "If I look like a trusting person, soon I'll feel like a trusting person. When I'm confused and afraid, I just keep smiling, especially at church, because most of those people expect me to be spiritually mature—and they are the last people I would admit my fears to!"

⌀ PERSONAL INVENTORY

Take a minute to identify any of the disguises mentioned above that you identify with. After you've given that some thought, ask yourself the following questions:

- What is the "ache" in my soul that has never been filled?
- Are my disguises so much a part of who I am that I have never admitted (even to myself) the fears they cover up?
- What (or who) triggers a fearful response in me?
- Do I struggle with guilt over my fears?
- Am I afraid to give and receive love?
- Am I experiencing a sense of hopelessness?
- Do I *want* to change, or am I afraid to leave the paradoxical comfort zone of my fearful disguises?

✍ THE ANATOMY OF FEAR

In simple terms fear can be described as, "Anxiety and agitation caused by the presence of danger, evil, or pain; it is dread, fright, or a feeling of uneasiness, anxiety, or concern; it's to be afraid of somebody or something (real or imagined); it is to expect with misgiving, to be uneasy or anxious."[3] So what really happens inside my head when I'm afraid? When we analyze the whole process, it's easier to understand as a chain reaction.

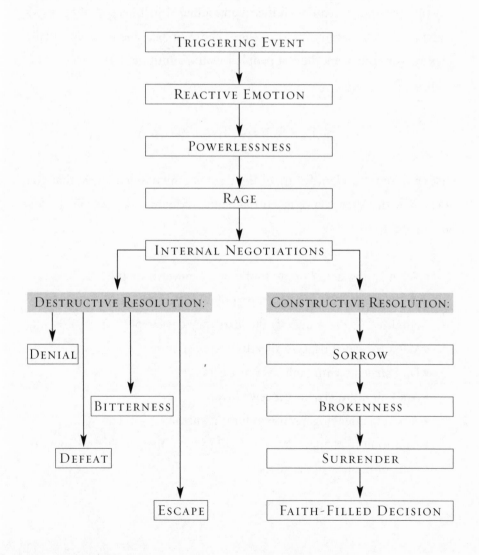

Triggering Event/Situation/Person

Something or someone is always the cause of fear. There is a "trigger point" that makes us aware of danger, evil, or pain. The cause might be from a real or imagined source, but it feels threatening, harmful, and disarming.

Reactive Emotion

Our first honest reaction to the triggering event is virtually involuntary. It might be the emotion of shock, terror, panic, dread, anxiety, horror, hurt, anger, or shame. Depending on our personalities, we have different initial reactions to the same events. For instance, one person might have a panic reaction that is immediately recognizable as fear. Someone else's first response might be anger, which could be displayed by a volatile outburst or by passive, wounded withdrawal. Although the initial reactive emotion may vary, fear is always what's underneath.

Powerlessness

After we have an intense, automatic, emotional response to an event, it doesn't take long to realize that things aren't going according to our plan. We feel alone and unprotected before a scary, powerful person or situation. We are not in control the way we would like to be or thought we were. Things are happening to us—or inside of us—without our permission!

This is a frightening feeling, and we aren't comfortable staying with it for long. We feel overwhelmed by what is happening, the way Peter felt when he looked around him at the storm. When our focus is on ourselves and our life circumstances, rather than on Christ, we realize we are pretty puny and helpless. If we were sinless, we would immediately turn our focus to Christ's sufficiency, but every human's natural tendency is to try to regain control first. So we move to the next stage.

Rage

The rage response sometimes begins with a feeling of betrayal. "Wait a minute, here. What happened to my safety and security? How can this be happening to me? I can't believe *that person* or *life* or *God* has let me down so completely!" At this point, sometimes unconsciously, we raise our fist in the face of God. We cry, "I hate what is happening here, and *I won't have it!* I refuse to feel helpless and dependent. God, You have let me down, and I can't trust You anymore."

This rage response may or may not feel like anger, but in essence, it's a posture of defiance (self-reliance) that is based on the fear that God can't be trusted, so we must go it alone in order to have things the way we want them. This is the nature of sin.

Internal Negotiating

Here lies the turning point in the whole chain reaction. The first four steps occur very quickly—almost involuntarily. Sometimes we are not even aware of every step. Once we have (1) *identified a trigger point*, (2) *experienced a reactive emotion*, (3) *felt totally powerless*, and (4) *responded with overt or subtle rage*, we begin (5) *internal negotiating*.

This is where we thrash around trying to come up with a way to fix our feelings or situation. It's our self-centered, determined effort to escape both our pain/powerlessness and the need to surrender to a Power greater than ourselves. At this pivotal point, we come up with our options: *Will we choose the path of self-reliance or the path of God-reliance?* Depending on our answer, we will "resolve" our fear in either a destructive (God-denying) way or a constructive (God-honoring) way. One of the two following courses of action will be chosen.

Destructive Course of Action

If we choose the destructive route, we'll get stuck in one of four "resolutions." None of these choices solves the problem or takes away the fear. All are rigid, dead-end choices.

Denial: A frequent reaction to fear is to deny there is a problem, person, or painful situation that must be dealt with. Even when our initial reactions to a triggering event are powerful, we are amazingly adept at climbing to the surface of life again, where we can pretend we aren't really angry or afraid.

Defeat: Many of us respond to fear with a posture of automatic defeat. We believe negative things have happened to us, causing our fears, and we have no power to change our feelings or life situations. We have no energy or confidence to take action and believe we can't handle our triggering event, situation, or person—so we give up. We play the role of a hopeless victim, squashed by life and by God.

Bitterness: Another popular response to fear is to look around and find someone else to blame—our parents, spouse, friends, coworkers, or even God. If we can point the finger at another person who is responsible for causing our grief, we can "justify" our paralyzing bitterness and delay any positive action toward resolving the fear in a God-honoring way.

Escape: Perhaps the most prevalent of all the destructive resolutions to fear is running away from reality. Many of us have become quite skilled at muffling our troubles in layers of compulsive/addictive behavior so we don't have to admit our feelings or deal with our fears. This choice denies God a chance to work and leads to perfectionism, legalistic spirituality, workaholism, codependency, or enslavement to a wide variety of mood-altering substances or behaviors.

Constructive Course of Action
On the other hand, if we choose the constructive route, avoiding the four dead-end choices, we allow our rageful, self-reliant thrashing around to bring us to our knees—and into a more honest, substantial relationship with God.

Sorrow: Sometimes we wallow around in a mental pigpen of betrayal, powerlessness, hurt, and anger for a long time. The turning point occurs when we stop trying to "fix" our feelings or situation and begin to grieve honestly and deeply. We live in a "groaning" creation where imperfect people hurt and disappoint us. That's sad. When powerful people abuse their positions and make us fearful, that's sad. When we are abandoned by someone we expected to love us, that's sad. But when we allow the sorrow of a sinful world to penetrate us, something else happens. When we cease playing the blame game and allow ourselves to grieve, we change.

Celebrate the moment! Horrible as it is, sorrow is the first major step toward a real solution. We have been betrayed. That's sad. We have felt powerless. That's sad. We have been profoundly hurt. That's sad. We've been angry and internally consumed with rage. That's sad. We aren't relating to other people and God the way He intended His children to relate. That's sad. But Christ promised that those who mourn will be comforted!

Brokenness: We are needy people. When we acknowledge on a deep level that we are much too impotent and unwise to resolve our problems and fears without help from a Power much greater than ourselves—God the Father—we are on our way to real healing. We can continue to respond with fearful emotions while we're walking on the uncertain waters of life. Or we can recognize the strength of the hand that He is already extending toward us and humbly acknowledge our need. We can say, "Lord, I cannot pick myself up by my own bootstraps. I need You." A broken heart is a humble heart, and a humble heart isn't too ashamed or self-reliant to ask for help.

Surrender: Surrender is knowing where to turn and doing it. It's crying, "Father, save me! I'm drowning in my circumstances. My fears envelop me. Uncertainties are everywhere. My past is a ghost before me. Father, forgive me for thinking I could solve all this on my own. Take away any false guilt I carry for the honest feelings of hurt or anger I have had or for what others have done to me. Help me to toss my extra baggage overboard. Teach me how to trust You."

Surrender can be a hard pill to swallow. It implies giving up my will. My plan of action. My fearful disguises. Taking off my masks. Revealing my need. Confessing my sin. Admitting that after years of serving Jesus, I still struggle with understanding the perfect love that casts out fear. With my surrender comes a willingness to be taught. To stop blaming other people and events for my fears and struggles. As I let go I feel lighter. Less weighed-down. More honest. Less compulsive.

Faith-Filled Decision: Once I let go of the situation, the person, the deep emotion of fear along with the potential consequences and implications and place it all in God's hands, I can decide to trust Him to take me through whatever lies ahead. I can face my past and accept the truth. I can reveal who I am to others and not be overwhelmed with shame or anxiety.

Something is different. It has to do with the mystery of my *fear of God*. He is awesome. He is holy. He is kind. He is good. He loves me. Beneath my meager understanding of Him is the knowledge that nothing can happen to me that does not have the potential for transforming me into His likeness and bringing glory to His name. No disgrace, hurt, pain, abuse, shame, embarrassment, or fear needs to be wasted. He can turn it to good.

A PERSONAL CHALLENGE

How can someone believe this assumption of a kind God at work in the middle of life's fears if she has never experienced and doesn't now know what His "perfect love" is? This book will address that question. The next ten chapters deal with specific fears many women share. I'm among you. A fellow struggler. Maybe you're in bondage to one of them too.

Don't be discouraged. There's hope just ahead. Take a risk. Step out of the boat and walk on the water. It is frightening at first. But when your eyes meet those of the Captain, your fear is diminished. Your confidence grows. Your faith is restored. When He reaches for your hand on the uncertain waters, look to Him, hold tightly, and don't be afraid.

PART TWO

OVERCOMING OUR TOP TEN FEARS

"WHY DO I LET IRRATIONAL PANIC IMMOBILIZE ME?"

Fear 1: Paralyzing Phobias

Severe anxiety disorders can exist even in loving
Christian homes. They are often the outcome of
strictness, misunderstandings, or miscommunication,
and they result in unexpressed anger and resentment.

KAREN RANDAU
Conquering Fear

Moonlit gravestones. Dark shadows. Eerie sounds. Stray cats. Sadness. Death. Funeral homes. Cars with flags. Somber faces. People crying. The year we moved to the house next to the cemetery produced the worst memories of my childhood. My second-story bedroom window faced the burial grounds, and the scene from that spot would send chills through anyone who struggled with fear. I knew I was a Christian and that heaven would be my final destination—but the process of dying and getting there always bothered me.

The panoramic view from the window was never pleasant or uplifting, but there were two horrible times to look toward the cemetery: when the moon was bright and when a group of mourners stood by one of those big holes in the ground. I'd pull my shade down, placing a tangible barrier between me and all of those dead bodies outside. But sometimes I had to look. And I was terrorized.

One glance out that window when the moon was full produced hundreds of shiny reflections off the grave markers on that well-used piece of property. And instantly I'd think about all of the decaying bodies in the ground right outside my window.

One evening I was put to bed early. Mom and Dad were entertaining company, and I knew I was not to interrupt the party the adults were having downstairs. I couldn't sleep, and hesitantly, I *dared* to peek out the window. The moon illuminated the entire graveyard, and macabre shadows dancing between the trees and the marble stones convinced me that *something* (or *someone*) ghastly was coming toward my window. Terror consumed me.

Quickly, I weighed the consequences between my father's wrath if I interrupted the party and my total inability to live with this gripping fear alone. I had a tooth that was slightly loose, but not ready to fall out on its own yet. I knew if the tooth came out, it would earn me the right to go downstairs.

With determination, I took a piece of string, tied it around my tooth, and secured the other end to the door handle. It took fierce courage to slam that door—but the desired result was forthcoming. My prize tooth and blood-stained pajamas earned me a ticket to the party below.

THE GHOSTS OF TODAY

I have often looked back on that stage of my life with a smile. After all, children are afraid of many imaginary ghosts. Certainly the power of imagination makes their fears far more exaggerated than any potential existing danger. But then I realize there are some days when I deal with fears that are just as debilitating as those I experienced from the bedroom window. Only this time they don't look like eerie shadows. Because I'm older and can actually identify some of the "gruesome goblins" of fear in my life, they are more obvious and, in many ways, more painful and paralyzing. I know I *should* be mature enough and wise enough to deal with my fears as a rational adult should, but I can't.

⚘ FOUR IMPORTANT FACTS

"What are you afraid of?" I have asked hundreds of women that question, and the answers range from bugs to unemployment, public speaking, water, high places or crowded places, to abandonment, intimacy, getting trapped in the wrong marriage or the wrong job, dealing with the past, to failure or success, and back to spiders, flying, the dark, the process of dying and facing death, or the unknown. And the list goes on.

I soon came to the conclusion that (1) *all women fear something.* It took a very short time to realize that (2) *some women fear more than others. Nation's Business,* in an article titled "How to Turn Off the Anxiety Alarm," stated:

> One moment you're fine. The next, you're gripped by a terror so overpowering you feel as if you're going to die. In 10 or 15 minutes that sense of impending doom passes, leaving you limp, exhausted, and wondering what happened.
>
> Panic disorder, which affects up to 2 percent of the U.S. population, is characterized by chest pain, shortness of breath, dizziness, sweating, trembling, and a racing heart. The all-consuming anxiety typically causes sufferers to think they are having a heart attack—or going mad.[1]

The article went on to quote the National Institute of Mental Health, saying that "approximately 10 percent of all people will have a panic attack at some time in their lives. But victims of full-blown panic disorder can experience four or more panic attacks every month. One-third may become so enslaved by their affliction that they develop agoraphobia—fear of going into open places."[2]

Thinking back to the panic attacks I occasionally experienced in the bedroom next to the cemetery, I remember feeling momentarily disabled, unable to think rationally, and totally panic-stricken—but I soon realized I would live. When women experience severe panic they are not always convinced they will be able to go on functioning as "normal" human beings.

My next conclusion was that (3) *some women remain frozen in fear for much of their lives.* Then I found an article titled "Phobias, Panic, and Fear—Oh My!" and I discovered how widespread the problem really is.

If panic fills your heart every time you approach an airplane or a tall building, join the club. Recent studies conducted by the National Institute of Mental Health in Rockville, Maryland, indicate that anxiety disorders are the number-one mental-health problem among American women. In fact, panic, anxiety and phobias interrupt the lives of nearly 20 to 30 million people in the United States.[3]

The more I studied, the more I realized that while totally debilitating panic attacks may affect only 2 percent of the population, milder versions of paralyzing phobias hit most of us at some time or another, and they are more frequent and intense in the wake of September 11, 2001. In fact, if we each looked back on the past couple of weeks, we could probably list one or two examples at this very moment.

So what makes the difference between the woman who becomes

immobilized by fear and the woman who experiences various forms of panic, anxiety, and worry but is able to remain functional and even productive in her daily life? I finally realized that (4) *each woman can choose a constructive or destructive resolution to her fears.*

For a moment that thought bothered me. What about the woman confronted with fear who instantly gets negative physical symptoms—a racing heart, sweating, heavy breathing, pain in the chest, trembling, and dizziness? It seemed unfair to suggest that she could choose a different path when her symptoms were so automatic. However, each of us *does* have a choice. Will we remain frozen in a no-win situation, or will we get help for a constructive way of dealing with paralyzing phobias?

As I pondered my conclusions, they felt right.

1. *All women fear something.* It's normal and even healthy to have some fears. We are not alone. Millions of women have dealt with some of the same fears we face every day.

2. *Some women fear more than others.* A few of us, due to past issues, struggle with fear at a much deeper level than others. This does not mean we are strange, unChristian, or in need of institutional care. It's a fact of life.

3. *Some women remain frozen in fear.* You may have picked up this book because that statement describes you right now. The paralyzing phobias in your life have placed you in a prison of misery and hopelessness. There are days when you are convinced *nothing* can change your current situation, and at times you feel like giving up.

4. *Each woman can choose a constructive or a destructive resolution to her fears.* Hope is tied to the belief that a change for the better is in the future. God created us with the ability to choose, and He offers us the opportunity to make important decisions every day. As one person noted, "Though no one can go back and make a new start, anyone can start from now and make a brand new end."[4] It's never too late.

⅓ A PEEK IN THE BEDROOM WINDOW

My triggering event/situation/person: Looking back at my crippling panic, I know the event that triggered my fear was the move to the house next to the cemetery—along with the bedroom with a far-reaching view of the gravestones.

My reactive emotion: Even though I knew the process of dying was a normal function, my heart failed me when I thought of bodies in caskets, vaults in the ground outside, and bodies coming out of those graves. My consuming emotion when I looked out at the dark cemetery was *horror.*

My powerlessness: As a child who wanted to trust God, I had a dilemma. I prayed God would take away the fear. But He didn't. I was the oldest of several children, and there were no extra beds in other rooms. I was stuck in a no-win, paralyzing situation. To leave the room was to disobey my parents. To stay in the room was to face the ghastly fear of whatever was beyond the window. My total focus was on my personal pain and my inability to change the circumstances.

My rage: Sometimes I felt angry. I was sure my father did not understand the depth of my fear. He thought I was a big baby who had to get used to the new house. My dad was a soldier in World War II, and death was a fact of life. He loved me deeply, but he was also convinced that I would get used to the cemetery and overcome my "silly fear." At that time in my young life, I didn't realize rage was brewing, but it was. I was *not* a big baby. I was deeply afraid of the dark, of death, and of unknown monsters on the other side of the windowpane. I was furious!

My internal negotiating: Even at the age of six I had a strong natural bent toward self-reliance. There *had* to be a way to take care of my problem. The fear was more than I could bear. On the specific night I described, my internal negotiating led me to an escape—extracting a tooth—so I could have a legitimate reason to leave the room and run from my paralyzing panic to safety.

My choice: After choosing a dishonest resolution to my fear, I had to face some facts. If I pulled out a tooth every time I needed to escape from my fears, I would soon run out of teeth. I needed a more constructive resolution.

My sorrow: I knew my mother understood the depth of my fear. In years past I had run to her side of the bed when I awoke in the middle of the night with nightmares. She always put an arm around me and let me fall asleep in her bed before Dad got up and placed me back in my own bed, long after my fears were quieted. One day when we were alone in my room, Mama looked out the scary window with me. With tears in my eyes I admitted how frightened I was. She didn't laugh at me. She grieved with me and felt my sorrow as her own.

My brokenness: When my mother began to realize how debilitating and gripping my fear of the cemetery was, we talked together—and to God— about the panic I was feeling. With deep emotion I told God I couldn't handle it anymore. The fear consumed me, and I felt helpless before it.

My surrender: After I poured out my heart to God, Mama got out "The Promise Box." It was filled with little cards with Scripture verses on them and a "thought for the day." The box always could be found on the kitchen table, and every day after our evening meal, one of the six children in our family would have a turn at picking a new promise.

On this day Mother permanently removed one of the promise cards. She read to me, "When I am afraid, I will trust in you" (Psalm 56:3, NIV). She talked to me about how fear can be a friend that causes us to reach out to God. She said how difficult it would be to understand what it means to trust God if we never experienced a fearful emotion. That day I surrendered my phobia to God.

My faith-filled decision: On the day I surrendered my fear to God, Mama placed the promise card in my hands and folded my fingers around it. Many times I felt afraid for a while, but I never returned to my former debilitating panic. From that time on, the card was always under my pillow as a reminder that I was not alone. And when the moonlight danced on the marble stones, I held the card—and I felt safe.

Larry Richards describes what I learned:

> How is fear a friend? Fear is a friend because it is only when we are afraid that we plumb the depths of trust. We cannot know what trust means unless we live through experiences in which the Lord is all we have to hold on to. Through his experience of fear, David became able to share a great and wonderful discovery with us,
>
> > When I am afraid,
> > I will trust in You.
> > In God, whose Word I praise,
> > In God I trust; I will not be afraid.
> > What can mortal man do to me?[5]

WHEN DOES A FEAR BECOME A PHOBIA?

None of us wants to be paralyzed by a phobia. But it happens. Most of us at some time struggle with illogical fears. And if there is a legitimate cause for the fear, we may magnify the potential problem beyond logical reason. Webster's dictionary defines a phobia as a "morbid and often irrational dread of some specific thing."[6]

An article in a well-known women's magazine, titled "Scare Tactics—Living With Your Secret Fears," stated,

> What are you afraid of? When we asked that question around the *Mademoiselle* office, the replies ran the gamut. . . . In short, everyone's scared of something. Which isn't really a problem—

unless it develops into a fear that's irrationally out of proportion to the actual danger and so intense that it starts interfering with your daily life.[7]

That's the best definition of "phobic fear" I've found! I began to think of the women I'd met who experienced varying stages of fear. In the beginning, many of our fears are normal, self-protective emotions. But when our fear gets totally out of proportion to the actual danger—and when we let the fear interfere with our daily schedule—the fear becomes a phobia.

Sometimes paralyzing fears are based on things that *might* happen. In the scenarios that follow, remember that each of us has a choice: Will we stay frozen in fear, allowing our phobia to get out of proportion to the actual danger, or will we move forward?

Losing someone we love: Jenny panics when she thinks of the possibility that her mother will die. Her mom has always been there for her— through an unhappy marriage, financial problems, and a major health crisis. Though her mom is in good health, Jenny is consumed with anxiety about losing her.

Aging: Sharon is afraid of getting older. As a young woman she won several beauty contests, and she feels that her worth is tied to her appearance. As fine lines appear around her eyes and lips, Sharon is absorbed in irrational worry about her dissipating value to others.

Being raped: Judith is a professional woman who is sometimes paralyzed by the fear of being raped in her apartment building. She finds it difficult to unlock her front door after dark.

Terrorism: Heather is a new mother and the thought of raising children in a world where suicide bombers can penetrate our national security terrifies her.

Loss of financial security: Jane's husband is a stockbroker, and she knows there will be layoffs at the firm. Her home is exquisite, but there's a high mortgage. And with two children in college, her worst fear is the potential financial devastation that could be just around the corner.

These brief vignettes remind us that many of our fears are tied to things that have not physically touched our lives yet—although they might happen in the future. Some of these fears have not reached the phobia stage yet, but they are beginning to alter our behavior on a daily basis. We start planning ahead to avoid certain places, people, or events. Sometimes the change in our behavior is so gradual we convince ourselves we do not have a problem. Phobic fears often follow a destructive path, and we wind up (sometimes unconsciously) choosing one of the following false resolutions: (1) denial, (2) defeat, (3) bitterness, or (4) escape into compulsive/addictive behaviors.

⅗ FROZEN IN A SEA OF HOPELESSNESS

When a triggering event produces a reactive emotion of fear that develops into an irrational panic, it is easy to feel powerless. We then move to rage and on to internal negotiating. We get stuck in beliefs and reactions like these:

- I am powerless to change my fearful situation.
- There is nothing I can do to alter my losing reaction to fear.
- I am so angry at the person who triggers this fear in me!
- I am so mad at myself for this embarrassing and emotional reaction.

When we choose to remain frozen in a sea of hopelessness, our internal negotiating often leads to thoughts like these:

- I will have feelings of panic, extreme discomfort, worry, and anxiety until I die.
- I can't handle my fears, so I'm giving up on trying.

- If I had more supportive people in my life, I'd be able to let go of my fears.
- I refuse to admit I have a problem. If I work harder, I'll forget my worries.

In every case, paralyzing phobias lead us to a poor quality of life, a sense of being trapped inside our own skin, and a defeatist attitude that does not make room for wise counsel from friends or professionals or for any thought of choosing another path. Simply stated, we say, "I quit!"

Nicky Marone, an educational psychologist and seminar speaker, writes of "learned helplessness" in her book *Women and Risk: How to Master Your Fears and Do What You Never Thought You Could Do:*

> Many of us . . . live a secret life, which . . . is kept hidden from others. It is in this secret life that we understand the meaning of helplessness. It is in this secret life that we can be held in the grip of repetitive and destructive behavior patterns. We may hold steadfastly to unhealthy love relationships; we may struggle endlessly with eating disorders or substance abuse; we may panic needlessly at the unforeseen changes in our lives. Depression stalks some of us like a samurai. Many of us scrupulously avoid risk or challenge in any areas but the ones in which we have already succeeded, fearing the process of learning a new task. Even after achieving most of our goals, many of us remain plagued by the secret self-doubts of low self-esteem. . . .
>
> We bear an unnecessary burden, which undermines our ability to take risks and act in our own best interests. . . . We suffer from a condition shared by many women . . . a condition known as learned helplessness.[8]

Women are not the only people who match this profile, but we tend to assume fearful behaviors are a "gender" response. Instead of learning a constructive way of dealing with our fears and acting on an empowerment that is already ours if we tap into divine resources, we allow ourselves to fall into old patterns. False resolutions to fear often propel us into silence, depression, subservient compliance, and addictions—sometimes in the name of being a "good Christian woman."

✍ LESSONS FROM MOSES

I believe Moses had a phobia about public speaking. God had called him to lead the children of Israel, and his reason for being less than enthusiastic gives us some clues to his apparent fear.[9]

Moses said to God, "Who am I that I should go to Pharaoh, and that I should bring the children of Israel out of Egypt?"

So God said, "I will certainly be with you."

Guess what! Moses was told ahead of time that he would be supernaturally empowered by God Himself for this awesome task. Then Moses said, "But suppose they will not believe me or listen to my voice; suppose they say, 'The LORD has not appeared to you'"?

We aren't told in Scripture if Moses' phobia had reached a paralyzing state, but it's easy to envision emotion in his tone. Moses said, "O LORD, I have never been eloquent, neither in the past nor since you have spoken to your servant. I am slow of speech and tongue." Can you *feel* the panic in his voice? He fears the place of leadership, and he is convinced his communication skills are the worst!

The Lord said to him, "Who gave man his mouth? Who makes him deaf or dumb? Who gives him sight or makes him blind? Is it not I, the LORD? Now go; I will help you speak and will teach you what to say."

I can almost hear God saying, "Moses, leave your low self-esteem and fear behind. Refuse to accept a resolution of denial, defeat, bitterness, or escape. I will *empower* you beyond any human level to do My work and accomplish your life purpose. My greatest joy would be to see you trust Me enough to make a faith-filled decision to overcome this fear."

Yet, after all that, Moses responds, "O LORD, please send someone else to do it." I believe Moses was very near a destructive, rigid resolution of total defeat. If we had a tape recording of his thoughts, the playback might sound like this: "Please, Lord, pick my brother for this job. I am powerless to change my fearful situation, and Aaron is a much better speaker than I am anyway. It's his gift! There is nothing I can do to alter my reaction to this fear. I will have feelings of panic, extreme discomfort, worry, and anxiety every time I stand before a crowd. I can't handle my fears, so I'm giving up on trying."

Fortunately, Moses' story doesn't end here. In fact, after he accepted the dreaded job of leadership, he became a powerful leader and an empowered, confident communicator. Acts 7:22 records that Moses was "mighty in words and deeds" (NKJV).

If Moses had chosen the *destructive* path of giving in to this phobia, the chain reaction might have looked like this:

Triggering event: God selects Moses for a huge leadership position.

Reactive emotion: Fear — "Lord, I've never been eloquent."

Sense of powerlessness: "O Lord, please send someone else to do it."

Rage: Moses could have said, "I'm upset! If God wants me to lead, He should have given me different gifts. This is unfair."

Internal negotiating: I wonder if Moses rationalized, "I can handle this situation myself. I'll get my brother to do the talking. He has a flair for putting words together so people understand what he means to say."

Choice of a destructive resolution: Moses could have selected either of the following options: (1) *Defeat*—"I give up! I've never been good at

speaking and I never will be. I'm defeated and I know it!" (2) *Escape*—
Moses could have turned to addictive workaholism and perfectionism, trying for a lifetime to make up for giving in to his phobia and turning his
back on God's call and God's enabling.

The Bible doesn't tell us in detail what happened at this point, but I
believe that the constructive path Moses selected in time made all the difference. The steps are the same in the beginning: *triggering event, reactive
emotion, powerlessness,* and *rage.* But his *internal negotiating* might have
allowed him to see a more constructive resolution for his fear. Perhaps the
scenario went like this:

Internal negotiating: Moses might have said to himself, "From my
experience as a believer, I know God never calls people to a task without
enabling them to accomplish the mission. I don't know how He'll be able
to use me, but I'm willing to try."

Scripture does not outline the emotional stages Moses went through
after God showed him miraculous signs and encouraged him by saying,
"Now go; I will help you speak and will teach you what to say." What we
do know is that there came a time when Moses' faith-filled decisions were
respected by all and honored by God. That leads me to believe Moses experienced *sorrow*. ("Lord, I wish I could speak with greater conviction and
clarity. My fear makes me ill every time I have to talk in front of people. I
feel so inadequate as a leader.")

I wonder if Moses then moved to brokenness. ("Father, in myself, I
can't do the job. I give up trying to manipulate people, situations, and
Your will. I can't do it anymore.") This kind of attitude always leads to
surrender. ("God, it's not my will; it's Yours! I desire to be Your servant
in the way You choose to use me. My focus is now on You, and I give
my self-reliant will up to You.") This attitude always leads to *faith-filled
decisions*.

⅃ A LOOK BACK THROUGH THE BEDROOM WINDOW

My greatest childhood phobia had to do with the "death" outside my bedroom window. As I became an adult, I struggled with Moses' problem—public speaking. Throughout our lives there will always be moonbeams dancing on the grave markers of life, reminding us of immobilizing fears. If our focus is not on God, we will feel powerless and full of rage. It will become easy to fall into denial, defeat, bitterness, or some type of escape.

But if we release our self-reliant patterns and learn to choose a constructive resolution for our fears, the benefits will be overwhelming.

God has given me a choice—*stay frozen* or *get moving* toward taming my fears. Instead of getting stuck in the process, I can choose to get help. Instead of waiting for assistance to come to me, I can pick up the phone and ask. Instead of blaming my mother, father, siblings, or church members for not giving me more assistance, I can take the initiative.

The surprising result is that a yielded inner spirit always leads me to feel grief for the phobia that has held me in bondage. This sorrow brings me to brokenness before God. As I yield my will to Him and experience true surrender, I find strength for my current situation that I never had before. And with that strength I am empowered to make faith-filled decisions.

An Epitaph to Strive For

As an adult, I now look at gravestones with a new attitude. Instead of seeing death, I see hope for eternity. Instead of concentrating on the end of this life and the process of dying, I look to my future in a place without fear. Instead of dreading the night, I look to the morning.

VIRGINIA VERDIER ALLEN

She never lost her sense of wonder, approaching each day as a surprise package to be opened with enchantment.

1917-1974

This stone marks the grave of Virginia Allen in Mackinac Island Cemetery. I have a feeling Virginia, who died at the age of fifty-seven, learned how to process her fears in a constructive way, which freed her to look to each new day with hope and anticipation. May we all learn to see with her eyes.

"WHY DOES THE FEAR OF THINGS THAT MIGHT HAPPEN CONSUME MY MENTAL AND SPIRITUAL ENERGY?"

Fear 2: Potential Disasters

It ain't no use putting up your umbrella till it rains.

ALICE CALDWELL RICE

The young mother was frightened. She had waited to talk with me privately after the meeting was over. "Carol, I don't know what to do. I have three children. My husband just lost his job, and we're living on unemployment compensation.

"My oldest son will start kindergarten next fall, and most of the people in our church think the public schools are corrupt and full of drugs and anti-God teaching. We can't afford the tuition at the Christian school in our area, and I know I am not cut out to homeschool my children. I just don't have the patience for it! I am so afraid my son will turn away from God if I send him to a public school."

The young mom was like many others I had met—afraid of so many things that haven't happened yet. I thought of my own fears. My child wasn't starting kindergarten, but in a strange way, I identified with this woman. My son was about to enter adulthood. Free to make his own choices. Free to make his own mistakes. And free to follow his own dreams.

A "SUMMIT" EXPERIENCE

As the mother of an only child, I've been a bit on the overprotective side. Sending a sixteen-year-old all the way to Colorado for three weeks of camp seemed like a big step. We had heard of a Christian leadership training camp called Summit Ministries—and it sounded like it provided a unique combination of high adventure and solid teaching. I tried not to be too emotional at the airport as we said our good-byes. By my standards, Jason seemed too young to be flying by himself.

Fear gripped my heart. What if he couldn't find his connecting gate in Kansas City? What if the camp didn't have transportation at the airport in Colorado Springs and he was left alone? What if he fell in love with a girl who lives on the other side of the country? What if he met older students who influenced him in negative ways?

When our son returned home, he was different. More mature. Less interested in video games. More involved in making plans for his future. He began talking about the importance of having a "Christian worldview" in the midst of our changing society.

Guardedly, he said, "Mom, what would you think if I told you I'm interested in a military career?" I could feel a lump forming in my throat. This child was special. He was intelligent, dynamic, full of fun and adventure, and he had a heart for the Lord. Why would he even think of going in that direction? I tried to follow my own advice to others. I listened more than I talked and waited for him to finish his sentences before opening my mouth. He handed me the journal he had written during camp, and my eyes fell on these words:

August 10

I prayed to God today about my future plans. I told Him of all my desires and asked for them within His will. I cried after I prayed because it was so intense. I wish all my prayers were like this.

Leadership was the center of the prayer, and it's my lifelong goal. I would like to lead our nation back to God, try to correct the wrongs, and make God first in all things. God has shown me His influence in every area of life that I see. "Lord, I want to be used by You in the work that You have set apart for me since my birth . . . and with the desires You have placed within me, I believe that You are leading me toward military leadership, or maybe even toward politics."

As I read to the end, my eyes filled with tears. My little boy had become a man. Fear was starting to choke me. Only yesterday I was putting him on the bus for kindergarten.

Thoughts swirled through my mind. Could it be that *God's* plan for my son might not be *my* plan? Could God's plan involve faraway places and the coarse atmosphere of a military compound? Had my son been unduly influenced by science-fiction novels and spellbinding movies? Or could these "desires of his heart" actually have come from God?

He continued, "Mom, I'd like to apply to the U.S. Naval Academy in Annapolis, Maryland. It's one of the finest engineering schools in the country, and I could get the best discipline and training in leadership that I could ever hope for. I want this more than anything."

13 "WHAT IF . . . ?"—WHAT WOMEN WORRY ABOUT

Most of us spend a portion of every day worrying about the "what ifs." We have an amazing ability to imagine the worst-case scenario, then we convince ourselves it *will* happen to us or to one of our family members or friends. An old Swedish proverb states, "Worry gives a small thing a big shadow." And worry eventually gives way to anxiety.

In *Conquering Fear,* Karen Randau wrote, "While *fear* focuses on an immediately impending danger (such as a car wreck about to happen), *anxiety* is a constant level of internal tension over something that may or may not occur in the future."[1] (I think I have just heard my own condition described.) Randau went on to quote Dr. Edmund J. Bourne, who said, "[Anxiety] is a vague, distant or even unrecognized danger . . . about something bad happening."[2] Anxiety brings a sense of apprehension, intense dread, and a dark shadow of uncertainty.

This chapter deals with the fear of "things that *might* happen." In the past ten days I have heard the following comments from women who have struggled with this type of anxiety:

- What if I lose my job? The company is going to lay off more people, and I just know I'll be one of them.
- What if I have a car accident? I just know I'll be maimed or killed. I better not drive.
- What if the economy falls apart? What will happen to our country?
- What if I never get married? I always thought I'd be married and financially secure by now, but I'm not.
- What if I can't get pregnant? I want a child more than anything and every month my disappointment is deeper and I fear the worst— infertility.

- What if I'm a bad mother? How can I ever be sure I'm raising my children properly?
- What if my husband gets interested in another woman? He's so attractive and I'm getting older.
- What if I can't afford to pay for my children's education? People can't make a living without a degree.
- What if we get transferred to another place? My whole world is wrapped up in this community. My family lives here. I just *can't* leave here.

Take a minute to write down all of the anxious thoughts you've had this week involving "things that haven't happened yet—and may never happen." Are you and I normal? Or are our lives unusually shrouded by a curtain of doom? Jane and Robert Handly, in an article titled "Why Can't I Stop Worrying?" state,

You wake up suddenly and look over at the glowing numbers on your alarm clock. It's three a.m.—again—and your mind is spinning with worries. . . . First, those Christmas bills you've got to pay. And what about the diet you're starting tomorrow? And how about your kids, your job, your marriage—the entire global economy? Before long, it's good-bye to sleep and hello to another red-eyed morning.[3]

These authors go on to quote a study which concluded that women are two to three times more prone to chronic worry than men are. It's true—all of us worry about some things. But how do we compare with other women?

According to a poll by Yankelovich Clancy Shulman, we're more concerned about the following issues than we were in the past: (1) money, (2) jobs, and (3) planning for the future.[4] According to a Gallup poll, women are the most worried about (1) the economy, (2) unemployment, (3) drugs, and (4) poverty and homelessness.[5]

If these studies are accurate, most of us are very worried about finances, employment/unemployment, and how this affects our future. We are also very worried about the impact of terrorism on our safety, our economy, and our emotional well-being.

The reminder of what I'd rather forget makes me feel depressed, defeated, worried, anxious, and fearful. For many of us, the fear of "something that might happen" slowly turns into a deeper level of fear that makes us feel as if our problem has escalated into a total inability to handle life, plan for the future, or provide safety and happiness for our children. If we aren't careful, we can even wind up saying: "I give up. The terrorists are out to get us. I can't do anything to stop it. My future is ruined. My family has no future. Fearful signs are everywhere. I'm going to quit trying!"

FIVE TRUTHS TO CONSIDER

Whenever I'm tempted to feel hopeless, I find it helpful to remember five simple truths.

1. *Life is full of negative things that might happen.* We can't escape bad news. It's on the front page of the paper. It's on the TV screen. It's in the conversations of people who surround us. We live in a fallen, sinful world. The Bible states, "We know that the whole creation has been groaning as in the pains of childbirth right up to the present time" (Romans 8:22, NIV). Life is hard, and it shouldn't surprise us that a fallen world will provide disappointment, painful losses, unfulfilled expectations, and sadness.

2. *As long as I choose a path of personal growth, I will face fearful situations.* The day nothing happens that makes us feel a little bit afraid, we'd better watch out! We may have quit breathing. Deceased people are the only ones

who never worry about the future or concern themselves with job security or financial reversals or their children's welfare. If you are making any progress at all, you *will* have concerns about what might happen in the future.

3. *Acknowledging my anxieties is a positive first step.* As a Christian woman, I have Someone to share my anxieties with. In the New Testament we are instructed, "Cast all your anxiety on him because he cares for you" (1 Peter 5:7, NIV). I can tell God anything, and He won't be angry or surprised.

4. *An attitude of optimism will make today more enjoyable.* One morning I hurriedly flipped on my radio. Chuck Swindoll was preaching and he quoted comedian Fred Allen: "It isn't good to suppress your laughter because it goes down and spreads your hips." I have no idea what Chuck's sermon was about, but that one comment helped me to forget for a whole day my "real" troubles and the fears over things that "might" happen in the future. Every time I tried to get serious, I laughed out loud.

Barbara Johnson wrote,

> Doctors and physical fitness experts tell us that laughter is just plain good for your health. One expert, who travels around staging workshops on how to be fit, says healthy people laugh 100 to 400 times a day. . . . I read about a medical doctor who calls laughter "internal jogging." He says that hearty laughter has a beneficial effect on most of your body's major systems—and it's a lot more fun than calisthenics. Laughing 100 times a day works the heart as much as exercising for ten minutes on a rowing machine.

Barb goes on to say, "One bumper sticker I saw [stated], 'ONE LAUGH = 3 TBSP. OF OAT BRAN.' . . . The best thing to do when feeling overwhelmed is to take 'laugh break.' If you're all worn out and feeling defeated, take time out to laugh. It can actually rejuvenate you."[6]

5. *Choosing a faith-filled decision is much less frightening than living with the underlying fear that comes from feeling helpless.* First, let's consider the bad news. Nicky Marone wrote, "Learned helplessness ensnares a woman in a tangled web of paralyzing beliefs, emotions, and behaviors. She consistently doubts herself even when she performs at consistently high levels. Superior achievement in one area of her life does not necessarily translate into high self-esteem or promote self-confidence in others areas."[7] It's important to ask ourselves if we have chosen to allow fear to paralyze us. We are in serious trouble when we start believing what we've been saying aloud when panic strikes: "I can't do anything. I can't handle this fear."

Marone continued,

> Criticism can so immobilize her with its implication of inferiority
> (which she already believes anyway) that she may scrupulously
> avoid new challenges, risks, or changes. . . . Fear and self-doubt
> short-circuit her attempts at change. . . . She eventually becomes
> blind to genuine opportunities to transform the areas of her life
> that make her unhappy. Learned helplessness becomes the grim
> reaper of her dreams.[8]

In my travels I have met numerous women who at first glance look like winners, but after talking to them, I realize they have chosen to be helpless victims of the fear of negative things that might happen.

Choosing a faith-filled decision might seem frightening, risky, impossible, senseless, stretching, gut-wrenching, and unnatural. But it's worth it! Old patterns usually feel safer, even if we've been miserable, than attempting a new method of dealing with fear. Sometimes we lose the approval of significant people—because it's chancy for them to risk losing us if we begin to shed the "helplessness" they still cling to. (We might not want to be in their support group anymore.)

◿ IS IT POSSIBLE TO UNLEARN OLD PATTERNS?

I have often wondered where worry came from. Did it begin with Adam and Eve, or is it a highly developed form of fear that we have "perfected" in the twenty-first century? Some women believe they learned it at their mother's knee. The authors of an article in the *Ladies' Home Journal* observed, "One woman stated, 'My mother had this great ability to create disastrous scenarios in her mind, and it rubbed off on me.' Some women told us that fretting made them feel they had some control over the dangers in life. By imagining the worst, they believed they could prevent it from happening."[9]

The article also explains that one of the biggest reasons women spend so much time worrying is because we have a "powerful nurturing instinct" that somehow makes us feel responsible for everyone. I don't think that's true of every woman I've met, but I *have* decided a whole book could be written on why we have this problem of worrying about things that might happen. But what I really want to know is: What can I do to change the pattern?

◿ DOES THE BIBLE HAVE ANY ADVICE ON THE SUBJECT?

One of the passages my mother encouraged me to memorize as a young woman was Philippians 4:6-8 (TLB): "Don't worry about anything; instead, pray about everything; tell God your needs and don't forget to thank him for his answers. If you do this you will experience God's peace, which is far more wonderful than the human mind can understand. His peace will keep your thoughts and your hearts quiet and at rest as you trust in Christ Jesus."

It sounds so simple. Kind of like the song Bobby McFerrin made popular several years ago: "Don't Worry, Be Happy." Pray about everything. Tell God my needs. Thank Him when I get answers. Repeat the pattern until I get peace. I want that! And God's peace will *really* keep my heart and mind quiet and at rest? Even if my son pursues a military career? Even if he lives on the other side of the globe? Even if I have no control over the circumstances? It sounds too simple. I've lived with fear so long I want a more difficult answer. I want to feel like I *earned* an answer to my dilemma. "God, why do I always want to make Your plan more difficult than it is?"

Jesus has more advice on the subject: "Give your entire attention to what God is doing right now, and don't get worked up about what may or may not happen tomorrow. God will help you deal with whatever hard things come up when the time comes" (Matthew 6:34). That must mean that worrying about things that haven't happened yet is a direct act of disobedience. God says every day that comes my way will have plenty of its own trauma, and I'm not to dwell on future "what ifs."

I'm not happy with this instruction. Part of my personality really *enjoys* worrying. In fact, it makes me feel mature to think ahead to all of the negatives in a situation. Who knows? Someone might appreciate my insight. But so far, I haven't met that person.

/3 ONE WOMAN'S STORY

Mary was young. Engaged. In love with a wonderful man. It must have felt like everything was going her way. Until the angel came. That was her triggering event! Joseph was to be her husband. Would the fear of a future event cloud their happiness? Would their carefully made plans be interrupted? Would they be exposed to public embarrassment and ridicule? What really happened?[10]

Triggering event/situation/person: The angel's announcement — "Greetings, you who are highly favored! The Lord is with you" (Luke 1:28, NIV).

Reactive emotion: "Mary was thoroughly shaken, wondering what was behind a greeting like that." I can only imagine the extreme panic Mary must have felt at that moment. Why would a heavenly being pick her out of the crowd for a special announcement?

Next comes the exciting "find" in the whole scenario! There is an interesting deviation from the chain reaction we have worked through in previous chapters. Most of us, even when following a constructive path for dealing with our fear, go through a feeling of *powerlessness,* followed by *rage*; we do some *internal negotiating,* which can lead us to *sorrow, brokenness,* and on to *surrender* and a *faith-filled decision.*

But Mary was different. There is a chance she experienced a moment of powerlessness. After all, she was vulnerable, exposed, and unprotected in the face of a startling announcement delivered by a heavenly being. There certainly is a chance she very quickly went through all of the steps internally, but after reading the Scripture carefully, I don't think so.

So what happened? I believe Mary's walk with God was so full of trust and her belief that the Messiah was coming was so strong that she skipped the usual pattern. The angel made the announcement: "Mary, you have nothing to fear. God has a surprise for you: You will become pregnant and give birth to a son and call his name Jesus."

Mary asked wise questions. "How could this happen?"

After the angel's explanation, Mary heard these words, affirming everything she already believed about her Creator: "Nothing, you see, is impossible with God."

Surrender: Without hesitation, Mary responded, "Yes, I see it all now: I'm the Lord's maid, ready to serve." With those words Mary released her own will and the security of her previous way of life and yielded to God's purpose for her.

Faith-filled decision: "Let it be with me just as you say." As I try to put myself in this young woman's shoes, I marvel at her lack of "what ifs." She was empowered with an ability to believe and trust, based on past teaching, which she knew to be true, experience, and supernatural confidence. She was embarking on a difficult road with more risks than most of us face in a lifetime—the potential loss of a fiancé who might not understand, friends and family members who might misjudge her, and birthing a son who would die the most painful death invented by mankind. We see no "learned helplessness" here. No second thoughts. No fits of sobbing or "begging off the assignment."

Mary teaches me that I, too, can practice a constructive way of dealing with my own fears and learn the value of "instant surrender" that leads to a positive, faith-filled decision. I'm encouraged to know that a time might come when I don't feel betrayed in the middle of my fear. There could come a day when, instead of choosing denial, defeat, bitterness, or escape, I move to a faith that says, "I trust You for tomorrow, even if the day is filled with uncertainty and trouble."

⅓ IT'S EASIER SAID THAN DONE

So how does Mary's story apply to my life today? She had a son. I have a son. One day Jesus was missing, and she found Him in the temple, sitting among the teachers, asking questions and interacting with the leaders, amazing them with His responses. She must have been as surprised as I have been to realize that her boy had become a young man. Too soon. Why, just yesterday he was playing in the carpenter's shop.

Jesus was filled with a sense of purpose. His future plans were set. "Didn't you know that I had to be here, dealing with the things of my Father?" (Luke 2:49). He was living out the plan God had for Him since birth. A plan different from what Mary would have wanted for her firstborn son.

Years later I look at this story through a mother's eyes and realize that my fears for "tomorrow" are well intentioned. I want to be a good mother, not a "worryin' woman." I want my son to fulfill God's purpose for his life, but I want it to be an easy path, without too many obstacles in the way. I find myself wanting to negotiate with God about these "desires" He's put in Jason's heart. I'm not good at letting go.

Sue Monk Kidd said it best: "Letting go is like releasing a tight spring at the core of yourself, one you've spent your whole life winding and maintaining. When you let go, you grow still and silent. You learn to sit among the cornstalks and wait with God."[11] I'm not good at releasing. I'm terrible at waiting. I'm even worse at trusting God for the "big stuff."

Perhaps the best way for me to end this chapter is with a personal prayer regarding my own struggle with facing what hasn't happened yet:

Lord, as I face an empty nest, I am afraid. I'm afraid for Jason's safety. I'm afraid he doesn't really understand what's involved in his choices. I'm afraid he'll be introduced to habits and language that are foreign to his protected life. I fear an unworthy woman may steal his affection.

Father, teach me that "letting go" involves a total surrender of my will and a faith-filled decision to practice what Mary said: "Be it unto me according to Thy word." Help me to affirm my son's manhood and trust his choices. Teach me to "be anxious for nothing" and to quit worrying about tomorrow.

Lord, with Your help, I will quit making my son feel guilty for growing up. Help me to stop depending on him to make me happy and to realize that only You can fill the empty places in my heart. I dedicated him to you when he was in my womb, and I affirm today that he belongs to You and is only on loan to me. Help me to look around and use my gifts to help others now that my hands-on parenting is almost over. Amen.

⅓ REVIEWING FIVE SIMPLE TRUTHS

As we work together through our fears, let's take a moment to reflect on the five truths discussed in this chapter:

1. Life is full of negative things that might happen.
   - Have I faced the reality of living in a fallen, sinful world, or am I still expecting life to be easy and free of pain?

2. As long as I choose a path of personal growth, I will face fearful situations.
   - Have I accepted the fact that saying yes to new opportunities and challenges brings numerous fearful situations that I must deal with?

3. Acknowledging my anxieties is a positive first step.
   - Am I so fiercely independent that I refuse to admit I need help, or am I willing to admit my fears to God and key people in my life?

4. An attitude of optimism will make today more enjoyable.
   - Have I added one humorous thought to my life during the last twenty-four hours? (To help you get started, ponder this: "The people who tell you never to let little things worry you have never tried sleeping in the same room with a mosquito."[12])

5. Choosing a faith-filled decision is much less frightening than living with the underlying fear that comes from feeling helpless.
   - If I have assimilated a pattern of "learned helplessness," will I

choose to face my problem and take progressive steps toward learning how to practice making faith-filled decisions in my daily life?

✐ MOVING FORWARD

In the next chapter I will confess my greatest fear—losing control. I know you already guessed I have that problem. It deals with my fear of vulnerability—and I'm encouraged to know I'm not alone.

"WHY DOES EVERYTHING I DO HAVE TO BE PERFECT?"

Fear 3: Losing Control

Control is an outgrowth of fear, insecurity and lack of self-esteem. The more anxious a woman is the more she wants to control and, conversely, the more secure a woman is the less likely she will need to control.

BARBARA SULLIVAN
The Control Trap

I've always been impressed by competent women. Intelligence, confidence, and a strong commitment to the work ethic is an attractive combination. As a young married woman, I selected a few "worthy" mentors and decided to become one of the super-achievers.

Average was a word I loathed. When I committed myself to a task, it was done well. I enjoyed tight schedules, impossible agendas, a full calendar, and demanding opportunities. After all, I believed God was worthy of excellence—and I always felt more spiritual when I was buried in work. I wasn't sure excellence, by God's standards, was defined by an insurmountable schedule and unrealistic workload, but godly people applauded my efforts and that only increased my desire to please them. Their affirmations and enthusiastic approval assured me I was selecting the right path.

⚡ LEARNED BEHAVIOR?

As the firstborn of six children, being "in charge" came naturally. I was the built-in baby-sitter, which made me the frequent disciplinarian of my four younger sisters and one brother. Dad always said, "The oldest person in the house gets to be the boss." Mother taught me to cook and clean at an early age, and I was convinced that "Cleanliness is next to godliness" was a verse in the Bible. I was also a charter member of the "Clean Up Your Plate" club.

Dad was the adult child of an alcoholic and had learned to take charge at a very young age. He valued strength, leadership, authority, personal discipline, obedience, self-control, and commitment to God. Dad taught me the following slogan: "Be a leader, not a follower; the whole world is made up of followers, but it takes a real individual to be a leader."

My early years were filled with strict Christian training, overflowing love from my precious Dutch mama, more than a little self-imposed fear of not pleasing Dad with high enough grades or noteworthy accomplishments, and a lot of work as I helped care for all of those babies who kept coming. I rather enjoyed being "Mom's right arm" and the big sister in charge of the little kids. Also, earning Dad's approval helped to mask my insecurities.

⚡ THE MAKING OF A PERFECTIONIST

My father accepted the call to pastor his first church when I was in junior high. After running from God's will for many years, Dad left a comfortable position in business, went back to Bible school, and finally moved our family to a little railroad town in Michigan. There were forty-two people in the first congregation—so everybody had a job. During my teenage years I was the church pianist, and later on, I functioned as the "acting" senior high youth director.

I started to love being in control. Leadership was natural for me. Mother and Dad were very busy with the young, growing congregation, so I was often in charge of my five siblings, meal preparation, and "media" control (phone, front door, and disgruntled church members). In my spare time I functioned as the program director and publicist for every event sponsored by my youth group.

Life was fast-paced. Men and women were coming to Christ through the outreach of my parents—and I *loved* being part of the ministry. As long as saying "yes" felt like a spiritual decision for a worthy cause, I accepted every opportunity, challenge, and invitation. I wanted to please God with my whole heart, and I secretly liked pleasing the people who told me how wonderful I was. I was also convinced that being "on fire for God" meant working harder and doing things more perfectly.

DEFINING THE FEAR

One of the most difficult fears to recognize is the fear of losing control. Why? In its early stages it looks so appealing. Women caught in "the control trap" appear to be dynamic, sharp, aggressive leaders—the "movers and shakers." They get things done. Their résumés are impressive and their lists of accomplishments are unending. Christian women who fit into this category are publicly honored for their commitment to worthy causes.

So how does something that looks so good become so wrong? Barbara Sullivan, in her book *The Control Trap*, asserts that few women set out to dominate their friends, coworkers, husbands, or children. But it's happening all the time. She says,

> One of the most widespread factors in a woman taking control is *fear.* Even though there may be legitimate reasons for the seeds of fear in us—a sensitive nature, past hurtful experiences, present unfavorable circumstances—what we *do* with fear as adults is our responsibility. We must see fear for what it is—a trap we fall into, causing us to subtly or overtly take wrongful control of the lives of those around us.[1]

Many of us who get entangled in this snare fail to see our problem until we are hopelessly addicted to the adrenaline of prestige and power. Even then, we tend to overlook the danger signs because of our obvious accomplishments and our internal belief that *no one can do the job as well as we can.* We don't see our mind-set as egotism. It's just a fact. We have deluded ourselves into believing that we are using our God-given giftedness to manage people, circumstances, and events in the best possible way, for the good of all concerned.

THE MANY FACES OF CONTROL

Since the fear of losing control is evidenced in many different ways with a wide variety of disguises, take a few minutes to read through the following list and ask yourself if you have ever assumed any of these ten controlling identities.

1. The *manager*—This person always leads every group she participates in. She is quick to volunteer and slow to delegate—because someone else might not do the job as efficiently or effectively as she does.

2. The *manipulator*—This woman's technique is so perfected that she gets people to do what she wants and they actually believe it was their own idea. Frequently the manipulator comes from a home where one or both of her parents were dysfunctional, so she learned to manipulate difficult people and situations at an early age—just to keep the peace and have the semblance of a normal life.

3. The *martyr*—The woman who controls situations and people "because no one else in the family will help" often becomes a martyr. Frequently, she "sacrificially" gives up her own rights and financial resources to meet the needs of others. Then, after all she's done for them, she controls them with guilt and obligation. Quiet, mild-mannered martyrs can control others with "the silent treatment."

4. The *meanie*—The woman who finds herself in this category knows she is a nag capable of intimidating the people around her. Known for her negative attitude about everything, she wears her family down by constant criticism. She controls by her forcefulness, browbeating, and policing of activities.

5. The *most spiritual*—Women who are married to nonChristians or "less spiritual" spouses sometimes fall into the trap of flaunting their organization of the religious training of the children. They do this in such a way that they subtly make their husbands feel like worthless, uncaring creeps for their lack of interest or involvement in church-related activities. Married and single women use their "spiritual prowess" to gain control in church and family situations.

6. The *mother of the extended family*—Women with honorable motives often control their children far into adulthood by "protecting them from serious mistakes" or "helping them to make right choices." Sometimes a firstborn woman (or one raised in a dysfunctional home) assumes the decision-making related to family reunions, care of elder parents, and the coordination of birthday parties and special events. She thinks she's doing it because no one else cares as much as she does. Later, she resents being left

with all the work and responsibility. This woman sometimes tries to "mother" her husband and robs him of masculinity and self-esteem.

7. The *most perfect person*—The most subtle disguise of all is perfectionism. Christian women try to achieve "excellence," which brings a pat on the back and a word of affirmation. The perfectionist has trouble delegating—no one can do things as well as she can! The perfectionist has trouble with fatigue—there are never enough hours in a day to get everything done properly. She has few close friends—people are intimidated by her workaholism, time constraints, and "superior" image. And she doesn't *allow* anyone to get close enough to discover her insecurity beneath the carefully constructed image.

8. The *mime*—This woman is not a "screamer," but she has powerful control over others by a certain look in her eye, the raising of an eyebrow, a grimace, or a body-language signal, all of which are understood only by another family member. The woman in this category could be reading this description right now and be shocked as she realizes (for the first time) she is exerting forceful control over her family members with this highly perfected technique.

9. The *morbid weakling*—Some women have learned to control by exhibiting physical or emotional problems. When a woman is ill, she becomes the center of attention. Family members change their plans in order to be close to her in her "hour of need." Often, she feebly tells them they don't need to worry about her, but she seeks to control their decisions by making them feel guilty if they don't focus on her needs before their own.

10. The *main attraction*—An insecure woman often learns how to control men by her feminine charm. As a child, batting her "baby blues" at Daddy always resulted in a "yes" to her requests. As she grew older, dating became a game, and when flirtatious behavior won the heart of a man, she moved on to the next challenge. Afraid of intimacy, this woman controls men by enticing them with her looks and childlike flirtation. She may

appear outgoing and confident, but fear keeps her from developing a mean-ingful relationship with anyone. Because women are not attracted to a woman exhibiting these behaviors and she rarely can control them using the same methods, loneliness becomes her companion.

⒔ WHAT DOES THE FEAR OF BEING VULNERABLE HAVE TO DO WITH CONTROL?

Looking at the list of disguises we sometimes put on to hide our fear of los-ing control, I admit I have worn several of these masks at different times in my life. Underneath my facade I was terrified of becoming vulnerable. Webster says the vulnerable person is "open to attack, hurt or injury; (has the capability) of being . . . wounded (either because of being insufficiently protected or because of being sensitive and tender); liable to greater penal-ties than the opponents."[2] That's me!

At the deepest level, I know opening myself up to other people, instead of controlling them, means I am vulnerable to letting them hurt me deeply. Instead of admitting that I have tender feelings, I'd rather choose a path of control, so I never have to give myself an opportunity to experience the potential pain in an honest, open relationship with coworkers or family members. In my youth, I observed a vulnerable rela-tive experience emotional abuse in the name of biblical submission. That wasn't going to happen to me! I was too smart to fall into that degrading and helpless trap!

When I was newly married, my problem with insecurity and low self-esteem was hidden behind a carefully constructed, aesthetically pleasing wall of perfectionism. Controlling my own behavior and that of others with my ability to manage everything well was the only way I knew how to pro-tect myself from disclosure. And no one guessed what I was doing. After all,

I was only carrying on with what I had done in my early years. Big sister Carol could organize anything. If my to-do list wasn't full, I questioned my worth. I was always focused on the next big project.

One day I was reading Paula Rinehart's book *Perfect Every Time* and realized she was a fellow struggler.

> When you live in the future you are always internally in motion,
> moving toward the next achievement, the next need to be met.
> You can be months, even years, ahead of yourself. It's a "when I
> finish . . . then" approach to life. . . . As long as I was immersed in
> a project or moving toward a goal, life had meaning and purpose.
> But as soon as a blank space appeared or my schedule eased up, I
> was more anxious than relieved. And the only way to address the
> anxiety, it seemed, was to get busy again.[3]

Paula's description of her cycle of anxiety was just like mine. Because of my inner insecurities, I wound up controlling people and situations in subtle but powerful ways, while demanding perfection of myself. When I saw flaws in my pattern, I would get off the "gerbil wheel," but I felt so worthless when I wasn't achieving, leading, and organizing that I soon resumed my former ways. Total exhaustion and a feeling of personal and spiritual failure eventually revealed my deception.

PLAYING GOD?

Dr. Chris Thurman refers to perfectionism as "the crushing weight of playing God." Most of us who fit the pattern of the controlling perfectionist would be appalled to be accused of trying to take God's place—but that's exactly what we work to do.

One of the primary causes of most psychological and spiritual problems is perfectionism, the belief that one can be just like God—all knowing . . . all powerful . . . and all places. What happens when most people run into situations they can't control? They respond with, "I'm going to do something about this!" They try to control the uncontrollable. What are they implying? Somehow, they should be so powerful that nothing should be beyond their control. Only God is that powerful.[4]

Once again our problem is rooted back in the Garden of Eden. Satan tempted Adam and Eve with the fruit of the forbidden tree by saying, "God knows that when you eat of it your eyes will be opened, and *you will be like God*, knowing good and evil" (Genesis 3:5, NIV, emphasis added). It's tempting to "bite the apple" and take the control of our lives right out of God's hands. We don't think of it as "usurping His authority," but that's exactly what we do!

For years my fear of vulnerability was hidden in a mask of false confidence. If I did God's work for Him, "helping Him out," maybe the pain of low self-esteem would go away. I didn't think I was "playing God," but my "I'll-do-it-myself" actions were demonstrating a lack of sorrow for my sinful self-reliance and certainly were not leading me toward repentance.

WARNING SIGNS

- When situations arise that need leadership, direction, and a "voice of authority," do I find myself mentally solving the problem and then jumping in to help, even if my advice or assistance has not been requested?
- Do I organize family events or take charge of family crises and later resent my siblings for not "doing their fair share"?

- Do I often feel like nothing will get done unless I take care of the situation or problem?

- Is it hard for me to enjoy a day off or a week's vacation? Is my mind preoccupied with the work I've left at home or at the office?

- Do I have trouble letting people get close to me emotionally?

- Do I focus more on the goal, product, or end result (the future) than on enjoying the process of getting there?

- Do I often set impossible goals and then mentally put myself down for low achievement?

- Do I feel uncomfortable disclosing my weaknesses and needs to other people?

- Would I rather not take on a project if my work couldn't be as good as or better than the last person who attempted the task?

- Do I get tired of controlling situations and people, but feel terrified of giving up the "status quo" and releasing my grip?

If you're wondering if you've entered the danger zone, check out how many "yes" responses you have to the preceding questions: If you answered "yes" to more than half of these questions, you and I have a lot in common! In my interviews with women prior to beginning this book, I became convinced that we have an epidemic of Christian women who have a fear of being vulnerable, which has catapulted us into a "tyranny of terror": If I give up my control, I will be weak, powerless, average, open to attack, exposed, and unprotected.

ELIZABETH'S STORY

Liz was one of the most capable women I had ever met. She was the Christian education director of a fast-growing church, wife of a busy doctor, and mother of three energetic, intelligent children. She and her husband had purchased a charming three-story Victorian home, which they had systematically remodeled and redecorated. With her talent, this woman could have done anything. She could manage, direct, teach, inspire, persuade, and create like no woman before her! Every time we were together I felt motivated to achieve new goals and serve God with greater fervor.

To my surprise, one day I received word that Liz had been hospitalized for depression. Could we be talking about the same person? Elizabeth, the achiever, church staff member, encourager, organizer, and supermom of three future leaders? There must be some mistake. But it was true.

After Liz went through treatment, we had dinner together, and she shared her story. Later, she put more of her thoughts on paper.

For me, clinical depression was waking up one morning in the fortieth year of my productive, Christian life feeling as if I had entered a foreign country. Something was happening to me I had never experienced before, and I didn't like it. One day I tried three times to measure and count four cups of flour for Christmas baking. My mind couldn't hold a thought. I could no longer concentrate.

I couldn't feel emotion. Even when my family took me to our favorite vacation spot, where we had spent our most precious family times, where I had always been drawn closer to God in the quiet and splendor of His creation, I could feel nothing. I was dying inside.

My job on the pastoral team at our church required compassion and sincerity, but I remember walking down the church corridor secretly wishing I could punch someone in the nose. On my days off I wanted to hide from people. Once, while shopping, panic struck—and I had to get out!

My confidence was lost, and I no longer had that valuable "passport to joy."

I was going through the motions with a smile on my face while I traveled further down into a place of sadness and despair. . . . There wasn't enough time to do all the "right" things in the day, so I began to rise in the middle of the night—every morning at three or four o'clock—so I could work. In the beginning, panic attacks woke me as my past fears surfaced in my sleep. In my slumbering state I was not in control enough to push the fears down again. As the panic attacks increased, it was easier to get up and work than to wrestle with my fears in the dark. But the fears grew.

As I continued reading Liz's words, I wept for my friend. She went on to describe how her coping strategies quit working. She had tried to serve God with her whole heart, and He didn't seem to be helping her. Maybe He didn't love her. Perhaps she was going crazy. She continued,

Since my conversion experience twenty years before I had never questioned God's grace. I had lived it, loved it, taught it, and shared it with undaunted childlike faith. Now, battle weary, lost, and helpless, my mind could arrive at only two conclusions:

1. This "God thing" and faith didn't work.
2. There was something basically not good about me. God couldn't love me. I was hopeless and I knew God couldn't use me. I was broken. God didn't want me. I had no value. God had forsaken me. I was not worthy.

This was the most terrifying moment of my life!

In a pool of tears, one night she expressed to her husband what was happening. With tenderness and deep concern, he made arrangements for professional help at a reputable Christian clinic. Liz said feelings of failure engulfed her as the former "supermom" waved goodbye to her three children as she left home for treatment.

⌇ CAN CONTROLLING WOMEN EVER BREAK THE PATTERN?

As we consider the development and defeat of fear, it helps to see ourselves in process.

Triggering event/situation/person: For both Liz and me, being firstborn children with high goals, expectations, and obligations, it seemed quite natural to cover our own low self-esteem and insecurities by "control."

Reactive emotion: Panic set in for me when I realized I could never work hard enough to make everybody happy. No matter how much I did, there was still more to do. I was afraid. After all I had done, I still wasn't feeling fulfilled and happy. I was afraid God would be displeased with me if I slowed down, but I knew I couldn't keep up the pace forever.

Sense of powerlessness: My fear soon led to an overwhelming sense of powerlessness. Paula Rinehart describes the feeling perfectly:

All of us who recognize ourselves as a woman "who does too much" hold this characteristic in common: We rarely realize how close to the edge we live until we have almost stepped over the line. . . . No matter how high your energy level, you can give for only so long without adequate replenishment. . . . It is God's way of puncturing the myth that you can make it on your own as a strong, independent woman who has no needs herself.[5]

Rage: Both Liz and I experienced an unconscious, growing, inner rage when we realized other people were using us because we were hard workers who always got the job done. When God didn't give us a continuing abundance of fresh energy as we continued to abuse our bodies and minds with work, it felt like He betrayed us too.

Internal negotiating: Controlling women are very good at internal negotiating. We convince ourselves that people who are as competent as we are shouldn't be struggling like this. After all, we don't really have a *problem,* we have a *challenge.* If we could just find a "how-to" book on more effective organization, or if we could find a better system for getting things done more efficiently, or if we could get by on fewer hours of sleep, we could resolve our fear of losing control. When we refuse to see that our total self-reliance is a sinful state, we are catapulted into a destructive resolution.

Destructive choices: I chose a destructive resolution of *denial.* Even though I saw danger signs, I was convinced I did not have a "big" problem. In his book *Imperative People,* Dr. Les Carter pointed out, "Imperative people just refuse to admit the truth—to others and sometimes even to themselves. They so strongly believe the lie that humanness is debilitating that they cannot bring themselves to admit even simple deficiencies."[6]

Liz, after a while, chose the destructive resolution of *defeat.* The God she trusted appeared to have let her down. Apparently, He didn't love her or want to use her in ministry any more.

Some women who are afraid of losing control choose a resolution of bitterness. They become resentful of the heavy workload that *always* ends up on their desks or the family responsibilities that continue to fall on their shoulders.

Liz and I both chose *escape into perfectionism* as our resolution for dealing with our fear of losing control. I continued in a pattern of workaholism. Liz wound up facing clinical depression. Other women choose a destructive resolution for their fear by escaping into eating disorders or addiction to alcohol, tobacco, or other drugs.

If Liz and I had allowed our internal negotiating to lead us to a constructive resolution, we would have honestly faced our fear of losing control and admitted it was a stubborn form of sinful self-reliance. We would have experienced genuine *sorrow* for our sin and for the misery of our lives. We had expected life to be easier, and we had anticipated rewards from God for working so hard. But the endless demands we placed on ourselves brought only emptiness. That was sad. Our growing perfectionism brought more anxiety into our relationships. That was sad. We both experienced a deep loneliness (even in the middle of crowds of people). That was sad. We felt alienated from God. That brought the most sadness.

This deep level of sorrow brings us to *brokenness* before God. Job knew what brokenness felt like and, in spite of all his losses, felt okay about voicing his emotions to God: "Though I cry, 'I've been wronged!' I get no response; though I call for help, there is no justice. . . . Those I love have turned against me" (Job 19:7,19, NIV).

Here lies that great challenge for the woman who is afraid of losing control: Our *internal negotiating* can allow us to convince ourselves we have no problem—which sends us right back to our escape into denial, defeat, bitterness, or compulsive behaviors. Or, it can lead us to genuine *sorrow* for the sin of relying on ourselves, instead of on God. David said it so well: "Generous in love—God, give grace! Huge in mercy—wipe out my bad record. Scrub away my guilt, soak out my sins in your laundry" (Psalm 51:1).

His sorrow led to *brokenness,* and then to *surrender:* "You're the One I've violated, and you've seen it all, seen the full extent of my evil." He experienced guilt, but he knew what to do about it: "I've been out of step with you for a long time, in the wrong since before I was born. What you're after is truth from the inside out. Enter me, then; conceive a new, true life. Soak me in your laundry and I'll come out clean, scrub me and I'll have a snow-white life."

True repentance always leads to *surrender.* It has been true for Liz. It was true for David—"God, make a fresh start in me, shape a Genesis week from the chaos of my life."[7]

The final step for all of us is a *faith-filled decision*. Liz chose to resign from her prestigious position in Christian education, to accept wise counsel from her husband, and to submit to treatment for her perfectionism, which had led to depression. She has fully recovered and now paces her life in a whole new way. She has time for her children's activities. She recently accompanied her husband on a short-term mission trip to Nigeria. She has time to entertain friends in her home. I believe Elizabeth's ministry is more powerful than it was when she was in bondage to perfectionism. She is relaxed, happy, and at peace.

I had to come to the painful decision of realizing that people will always ask me to do more than God asks me to do. I began saying no to worthy opportunities to speak when my calendar was getting full. In the beginning it was hard to force the words out of my mouth. When I was home for a day with nothing "important" to do, I would fall into old patterns of feeling worthless and vulnerable.

But I discovered something significant. Every time I made the *faith-filled decision* to release the old control reflex, I took a step forward. I began developing a "real" friendship, for the first time, with someone who held me accountable for following through with my decision. I learned how precious an intimate friendship is—no strings attached. By allowing myself to be vulnerable with another human being, I sometimes experienced misunderstanding or hurt, but the love I received so greatly outweighed the risk, I would never choose to go back to my old ways. I finally believe God loves me just because I exist, not because of what I do for Him.

The next chapter begins where we leave off here. I'm living proof there's hope for those of us who have denied our problem and covered our anguish with perfectionism and excessive work. Being vulnerable isn't easy. But it's a start. Old habits *can* be changed. Honest relationships can replace superficial ones. As we make progress, I think God smiles. He knows we'll be so much happier when we quit equating *doing* with *being*.

"IF I LET YOU GET CLOSE TO ME, WILL YOU STILL LIKE ME?"

Fear 4: Revealing Who I Really Am

*No one can develop freely in this world and find a full
life without feeling understood by at least one person. . . .
[She] who would see [herself] clearly must open up to a
confidant freely chosen and worthy of such trust.*

DR. PAUL TOURNIER
Quoted by John Powell in
Why Am I Afraid to Tell You Who I Am?

Abby was hard to love. In fact, Abby was even hard to *like*. Every time I tried to get close to her, she pulled away. And she never looked at me with steady eye contact. What was this girl trying to hide, anyway? Her body language begged for human compassion, but when I reached out to her, I was shut out.

My husband and I had accepted the invitation to become the youth directors at our local church. We were young university graduates with lots of enthusiasm and big ideas for redefining "effective youth programming." We accepted the challenge.

In the beginning, the job was fulfilling and rewarding. The group was growing. Eager volunteers were there to help out. Teens were coming to Christ. We felt successful and happy. But then frustration set in.

In addition to the normal exhaustion of a busy ministry schedule, we had a new problem that put us in a quandary. Our phone started to ring regularly at late hours. At first we thought the calls were a prank. When we picked up the receiver and said, "Hello," no one would speak on the other end of the line. After a moment, the caller would hang up. I finally figured out that the mysterious caller always rang our number after a youth event or church service — and I had a sneaking suspicion it was Abby — just checking to see if we were at home yet. The girl irritated me!

One day Abby confessed to me that she thought she was pregnant. I tried to mask my disappointment in this girl. After all of my attempts to help her, Abby always seemed to turn her back. She rejected every attempt I made to have an intimate conversation with her.

WHY AM I AFRAID TO TELL YOU WHO I AM?

Years ago John Powell wrote a book by that title, and the answer to the question reveals the total vulnerability of every one of us: "But if I tell you who I am, you may not like who I am, and it is all that I have."[1]

If I open myself up to other human beings and they laugh at me, ridicule me, or make my ideas seem unimportant and stupid, I will feel overwhelming embarrassment and shame. If I reveal something painfully personal and you handle the information carelessly or act like you don't really care, the emotional anguish will be more than I can bear. "Who I am" is all I have to offer another person. If you make me feel awkward and unworthy of your friendship, I may die of humiliation.

⅍ ABBY'S FEAR

My awkward relationship with Abby continued throughout her high-school years. At times I felt totally ineffective as a youth specialist because she rejected my attempts to get close to her.

She mysteriously "lost" the baby she was carrying. I couldn't decide if she'd had an abortion or if she'd made up the whole pregnancy story to get attention. Either way, Abby was not on my "favorites" list.

Years later a letter came from Abby, and she finally revealed her secret:

Several years ago . . . I came to you with the fear that I was pregnant. Do you remember? I need to explain to you the circumstances surrounding that situation.

During that time in my life I was being violently and repeatedly sexually abused. Because of the nature of the abuse and the threats that were ever present, I didn't dare tell you what was happening.

I hoped you would ask and prayed that you wouldn't. I was very scared. I could tell by your reaction that you were disappointed in me. I felt so ashamed because I knew what you must have thought. (Sometimes I still feel ashamed and dirty, but I'm working on that!)

I want you to know that I wasn't in that situation because I willingly slept around. I wasn't like that. If I had any control over what was happening, I wasn't aware of it. I thank God for pulling me out of that horrible situation. I was so afraid.

Her letter went on to explain that she had received counseling, was in a Twelve-Step program, and was busy working through the past so she could get on with the present and future. Tears brimmed in my eyes as I realized how wrong I had been about Abby. I had been totally blind to the nonverbal signals that were screaming at me.

⅓ BEING VULNERABLE—A RISK WORTH TAKING?

In the last chapter, we looked at the meaning of the word *vulnerable*. It seems to indicate the person who is "unprotected" emotionally or physically. When we feel like victims (due to past experience or current situations) we are particularly open to attack, hurt, or injury.

For those of us who have been victimized in the past, it's easy to fall into a habit or pattern of withdrawal in order to avoid the potential of being wounded again. After a while, we become convinced that we are susceptible to greater penalties in life than other people. This defeatist attitude is quickly detected by "users"—those who make themselves more powerful by selecting weak victims to control or hurt.

However, if we're honest, we must admit that sometimes *we are our own worst enemy!* Our minds have a tremendous capacity for exaggeration and distortion of truth. Sometimes we convince ourselves we have an aggressive enemy who doesn't exist.

But there is a flip side to all of this. Being vulnerable with the right people has the potential of bringing deep joy, emotional connection, and personal growth. To be vulnerable in the positive sense is to be accessible, innocent, and exposed. When we peel back the protective layers of our carefully crafted image and reveal ourselves to another human being who is worthy of that trust, true vulnerability brings an intimacy that breeds affection, transparency, tenderness, and understanding.

Fear 4: Revealing Who I Really Am 97

৶ SO WHERE DOES THE PROBLEM COME FROM?

If you have ever had a friend you tried to be open and honest with who clammed up and shut down every time the conversation turned to her personal life, thoughts, or feelings, you've asked the question: *What causes women to become emotional misers who are afraid to reveal themselves to someone else?*

After talking with hundreds of women about this topic, I've determined the fear of being vulnerable has many causes. Some of them are listed below. As you read through the descriptions, look for any similarities in yourself.

৶ TRIGGER POINTS THAT TURN A WOMAN TOWARD A CYCLE OF FEAR

LACK OF TRUST

Dr. Carla Perez, a San Francisco psychiatrist, says, "A lack of trust in others—usually dating from childhood—is the basis of the guarded woman's problems."[2] In an article in *Cosmopolitan* she goes on:

> Very early in life . . . this person was given good reason to conclude that she would be hurt if she let people know too much about her. . . . [This can happen when she] is condemned instead of comforted by her parents when she shows fear, ridiculed instead of praised for her dreams, or raised in a way that fosters intense mistrust of anyone outside her family.[3]

Lack of trust turns a fearful little girl into a grown woman who has great difficulty allowing herself to enjoy the luxury of intimacy with a spouse, friends, or other family members.

Shyness

Researchers have said that as many as 93 percent of all people have experienced shyness. We usually think being "shy" means we are quiet, timid, or fearful of interacting with other people. Psychologists sometimes refer to shyness as "social anxiety," and that can mean mild nervousness when you are around people all the way to the extreme of having a social phobia. Extreme shyness can hurt us in our job situations, love relationships, ministry opportunities, and in other aspects of our general social lives. It's very painful!

Low Self-Esteem

Years ago Dr. James Dobson wrote a book called *What Wives Wish Their Husbands Knew About Women,* and he documented a survey concluding that low self-esteem was the number-one problem of women. Sometimes early rejection by peers or family members is the cause. Another trigger point is repeated failure in everything from athletics to academics to career choices to relationships. Low self-esteem is an epidemic and is a major cause of our fear of revealing ourselves to others.

Max Lucado told a story of needing time to be alone during a busy workday. He found some "space" in a local cemetery during his lunch break (creative idea!), and he began wandering around, reading the engravings on tombstones. He came to one that said,

GRACE LUELLEN
SMITH

Sleeps, but rests not
Loved, but was not loved
Tried to please, but
pleased not,
Died as she lived—alone.[4]

Some of us will have more positive statements on our gravestones—or maybe just our names. But I wonder how many of us can identify with the unknown Grace Smith—the woman who tried to earn love and failed, tried to please people and didn't, and died emotionally lonely. Low self-esteem has nothing to do with economic status or level of education. It kills relationships, stifles creativity, and holds people in bondage to hidden fear.

SHAME

This category involves embarrassment, humiliation, abuse, and dishonor. Whatever happened in the past that brings a loss of reputation, painful memories, and repeated bouts of depression seems to keep us "locked up" in our emotions so we are unable to relate to other people in a healthy way. Dr. David Seamands wrote, "Memories involving times when we were deeply humiliated produce the most painful emotions we experience, and are some of the chief causes of . . . depression."[5]

MISSED OPPORTUNITIES

This category almost writes itself. How many times have you and I joined the millions of women who contemplate,

- If only I had selected a different career . . .
- If only I had married a different man . . .
- If only I had chosen to have children . . .
- If only I had more-perfect children . . .
- If only I had a chance for a university education . . .
- If only I had not come from such a dysfunctional family . . .
- If only I had a supportive friend/spouse . . .
- If only I had a church/denomination that allowed women to use all their God-given gifts . . .
- If only I were not trapped by financial problems . . .
- If only I had better health . . .

Lost opportunity can lead us on a destructive mental course. We begin to see that all of these causes of fear overlap and interweave. Lost opportunity can lead to low self-esteem. Constantly looking in the "rearview mirror" sometimes breeds humiliation or shame. The negative effects of missed opportunity multiply over time as we internalize and mentally magnify the fear connected with our regrets and second thoughts. Our frayed emotions lead us to poor interaction with people as we try to cover our hurts with an image of "I'm okay. . . and how are you?" Surface talk keeps us from appearing as unhappy, hurting, and fearful as we really are.

POOR COMMUNICATION SKILLS

I've spent years training Christians in communication skills through the "Speak Up With Confidence" seminars. I have met many women who are thinking, creative, educated, and attractive, but they are enveloped in fear when it comes to expressing what they know to other people.

But far greater than the fear of public speaking is the fear some people have of private, interpersonal speaking. Many women are convinced that every time they open their mouths, they can't formulate what they want to say in a meaningful sentence. Some struggle with getting their thoughts organized. Or they experience extreme nervousness in front of people they perceive as powerful. Others have been teased by siblings (or parents) about their strange gestures, word pronunciations, or oral mistakes. The majority simply believe they do not have the ability to share their thoughts in an articulate, clear, and concise manner. Rather than risk being laughed at or viewed negatively, they prefer withdrawal to the potential of public ridicule.

LEARNED INTERPERSONAL COMMUNICATION LEVELS

John Powell once stated, "To refuse the invitation to interpersonal encounter is to be an isolated dot in the center of a great circle . . . a small island in a vast ocean."[6] He began to study the way we reach out to each other and determined that most of us function at one of five different levels in our interpersonal communication.[7]

Level 5: Cliché Conversation

This is the "weather talk" level where we reach out to people on the surface, but say nothing meaningful or personal. "How are you?" "New glasses?" "Great outfit!" We appear interested in people, but never get past the superficial level.

Level 4: Reporting the Facts About Others

Career women and mothers are very good at this kind of communication. They say things like, "Have you heard about what happened to Jennifer?" or "My daughter is going to wilderness camp next week." At this level we offer nothing personal or self-revealing, but we do report the facts about other people, share gossip items, or engage in office chit-chat. It's still a very lonely level of communication.

Level 3: My Ideas and Judgments

This level of communication represents the first step out of the prison of "I'll talk to you, but I'm not telling you anything about myself." Women who risk communicating at the level of ideas and judgments begin to share a few personal thoughts, even some decisions they've made, but they are watching the "receiver" very carefully. Is there a raised eyebrow or grimace that would indicate disapproval? If so, it might feel safer to retreat to a less personal level of communication.

Level 2: My Feelings and Emotions

John Powell refers to this as "gut level" communication. At the previous level, as long as we are only discussing ideas we have, judgments we've made, or decisions that are forthcoming, we still have not revealed our hidden passions.

At this level we divulge what makes us feel strongly about our political persuasion, our child-rearing techniques, our commitment to issues or causes, and our approach to our faith.

For instance, I might make a judgment about you: "I think you are a very beautiful woman." There are many possible emotional reactions I might have regarding that observation. I may choose to share them with you—or choose to stay "safe." My potential "gut level" feelings are numerous. Keep in mind that my judgment is simply, "I think you are a very beautiful woman." But my *feelings* could have a wide range:

- ... and I hope my daughter is like you on the inside and out when she grows up.
- ... and I'm very jealous of you.
- ... and I feel good about myself when I'm with you.
- ... and I'd like to have your advice the next time I go shopping for clothes.
- ... and I feel threatened whenever you are around my husband.
- ... and I find myself putting you down so I can mentally elevate myself.
- ... and I'm usually intimidated by attractive women, but you make me feel comfortable and at ease.

Powell stated,

> Most of us feel that others will not tolerate such emotional honesty. We would rather defend our dishonesty on the grounds that it might hurt others, and, having rationalized our phoniness into nobility, we settle for superficial relationships. . . . Any relationship, which is to have the nature of true personal encounter, must be based on this honest, open, gut-level communication. The alternative is to remain in my prison, to endure inch-by-inch death as a person.[8]

Level 1: Peak Communication

All of us who have ever experienced an honest, truthful, authentic friendship have had moments of peak communication. Notice, I say, "moments," because with our human imperfections, we don't communicate at this pinnacle level every day. But when we share our heart and mind with someone who empathizes completely with our elation or grief, there are times of unexplainable oneness of spirit. It is the experience of knowing someone has "heard" us, accepted us, and felt our sadness or joy. We know a complete emotional and personal communion with another human being.

FACING THE CONSEQUENCES OF "THE FEAR TRAP"

As I talk to women who have chosen to retreat into the "safety" of not revealing themselves to someone else, I wonder if the consequences of that choice are far worse than the risk of facing the fear, feeling the panic, but making personal progress. Some of the negative results women have shared with me are listed here.

EMOTIONAL ISOLATION

Intimate conversation is the way most of us get to know each other, and it's an essential part of deepening a friendship or a marriage. When we deprive ourselves of gut-level communication with someone else, we become withdrawn and lonely. We are robbed of intimacy.

THE IMPOSTER PHENOMENON

Psychologists use the term "the imposter syndrome" to describe "a deep sense of fraudulence or unworthiness that bears no relation to reality."[9] When our sense of self-esteem is very low, though we may actually be educated, talented, and dynamic, we are convinced that we've gotten where we are only by fooling the rest of the world. We are fearful of letting anyone get too close to us—because they might find out what a "nobody" we really are and tell someone else.

Compulsive Behaviors and Addictions

When we internalize our feelings, we often give in to the destructive path fear takes. A lack of meaningful communication with anyone else leads to *a sense of powerlessness,* which fuels our *fearful emotion.* We react with a feeling of *betrayal,* then *defeat* or *denial.* The final step always seems to lead to the refrigerator, or perfectionism, or workaholism, or substance abuse, or to twisted perceptions of people and reality. We hate this destructive cycle, but we always seem to choose it.

A Fantasy World

The imagination is a wonderful thing when we dream the right dreams or engage in playful activities that come to life as our creativity helps us mentally to paint the picture of "what might be." However, when we constantly live "inside ourselves" with no opportunity to unload emotional baggage with a caring person, our mental pictures can breed untrue perceptions. We imagine that people aren't reaching out to us because we have a strange personality, or odd looks, or because we always make a fool of ourselves in public. This distortion of reality is magnified if we are struggling with a lack of trust in people due to the shameful events of our past.

Internal Rage

Emotions boil when some women who are afraid to reveal themselves to others observe happy, well-adjusted people interacting well with each other. When the fearful woman is around these "examples of perfection," a fuse inside of her is lit. She doesn't know if it's extreme jealousy or resentment.

An inferno of anger begins to build as she realizes how unhappy, unfrequented, and unknown she is. Internal rage finally exhibits itself in the form of ulcers, strained work and family relationships, severe depression, or inappropriate comments or outbursts.

Spiritual Defeat

Most Christian women have been challenged by sermons on the Great Commission, the passage at the end of Matthew where Jesus challenges His leadership team: "Go out and train everyone you meet. . . . Then instruct them in the practice of all I have commanded you. I'll be with you as you do this, day after day after day, right up to the end of the age" (Matthew 28:19-20). We don't need to be reminded that spiritually active Christians tell other people about their faith. And not only are we supposed to speak of our own personal commitment to Christ, we *should* be coming alongside young Christians and teaching them what we know about the Word of God and the faith-walk.

To feel like a social failure because of our inability to reveal our emotions and feelings to others is one level of defeat. But compounding that guilt is our knowledge that we aren't fulfilling Christ's command. We seem to be afflicted with mental and verbal paralysis when it comes to expressing our faith out loud.

13 THE SECRET POWER WITH PEOPLE

People were always bringing hurting friends and relatives to Jesus. What was there about Him that made Him so approachable? The Bible seems to indicate that it wasn't looks that made Him so appealing. What was the secret of His ability to relate to people so well? Close observation gives us the answer. Even before He opened His mouth to speak to individuals who came for help, He was already revealing who He really was in a nonverbal way.

The account of Jesus' life in the four gospels gives us the answer to His amazing power with people. Repeatedly the text reads, "He looked at him [her] with eyes of compassion." Within a verse or two, something else becomes apparent: "He touched them." Everywhere Jesus went He did those two things.

1. *He looked at people, showing He really cared about them.* Compassion always makes me feel like people are concerned about my feelings, emotional responses, and hurts. Instead of feeling threatened, I feel valued and loved. Usually that feeling comes nonverbally from someone before he or she speaks a word.

2. *He touched people.* Appropriate touch through a handshake, a hug, a squeeze on the arm, or a pat on the shoulder conveys a volume of meaning. It's a nonverbal way of making people feel comfortable and desirable. The woman who touches others with a warm greeting or affirming pat appears much more approachable and is perceived as a person of warmth. Intimidation is not present. Fears begin to melt away.

WHAT DOES THIS HAVE TO DO WITH OUR FEARS?

Most of us suffer from varying degrees of the fear of vulnerability. It's a risky thing to offer our inner life to someone who might not hold what we reveal with tender loving care. We long for intimacy, but we are afraid to be the first one to offer it.

When we finally conquer this fear, we often find ourselves on the receiving end of a relationship with someone who is just learning how to trust. The person may have experienced years of low self-esteem or feelings of shame. It might be someone who still struggles with communicating what she means, or perhaps she feels victimized by lost opportunity. We can choose to remain a victim of our fear, or we can decide to admit the fear and do something about it.

A great way to start is by following the example of Jesus, the Master Teacher. When we begin looking at other people with eyes of compassion, we see a myriad of other women just as frightened as we are. It's been a long time since they saw another woman look at them as if she wanted to reach out and communicate in a meaningful way. If we take the second step of communicating through meaningful touch, we are often surprised by the warmth of the response.

13 LOOKING BACK AT ABBY

Remember the teenager in my youth group? In her situation the *triggering situation* that initiated her fear was sexual abuse. Her *reactive emotion* was panic, followed by betrayal. Was she pregnant? Would people think she was promiscuous? People she trusted abused her. Her own youth director didn't pick up on her nonverbal cries for help. These emotions soon turned into a sense of *powerlessness*. As a teen with no place to go and no one to ask for help, she felt totally unable to change her situation.

It didn't take long for Abby's emotions to turn to *rage*. Why would a God of love have allowed her to become so deeply damaged at such a young age? Why didn't the youth leaders she tried to communicate with understand her desperate cry for help? Why did family members allow the sexual abuse to continue when they probably knew what was going on? Nothing about the entire situation was fair!

Her *internal negotiating* could have led her to a lifetime of compulsive addictions. Instead, as the years went by, she had the maturity to realize that we live in an imperfect and unfair world. Instead of giving in to the destructive resolutions of denial, defeat, bitterness, or escape, she sought counseling and gave herself permission to feel deep *sorrow* for the loss of her virginity by a violent act. She grieved over her loss of innocence and trust.

In time, this grieving led to *brokenness*. The brokenness she experienced was not caused by false guilt for what had been done to her.

Here's where a lot of us have problems. Because of the emotional response of shame that often accompanies sexual abuse, sometimes victims feel as if they have to confess sin. They're not sure why, but they feel dirty and guilty. Satan powerfully deceives them into believing they caused the problem.

We often spend a lot of time asking God for forgiveness for the wrong things. It's the willful dependence on ourselves (trying to "play God") that gets us into trouble. Abby discovered that when we repent of the sin of self-reliance (not shame inflicted by other people), it leads us to *surrender* to God's authority in our lives. And finally, we are able to come to the place where Abby arrived—*a faith-filled decision* to change the future with God's help.

I saw Abby a few weeks ago. What a difference there was! She looked at me with confidence and didn't pull away when I gave her a hug. There was a sparkle in her eye as she told me of her immediate plans for this year and of her hopes for the future. She briefly shared her feelings about the benefits of her counseling and the positive changes in her life.

As I said goodbye, I realized Abby had become a well-adjusted, happy, and outgoing person and was fun to be with. This "new" woman was open, honest, vulnerable, and accessible. She shared emotions and feelings. She was the kind of person I would want for a friend. Before I left, *she* looked at *me* with eyes of compassion and asked how I was doing in my personal life and ministry. Abby's gentle touch assured me she really cared and my heart responded to her genuine warmth.

A FINAL CHALLENGE

If you have been "locked up" and unable to reveal your feelings and emotions to someone else, will you face your fear and risk rejection in order to make progress? When you face your fear, say, "So what?" Ask yourself, "What's the worst thing that could happen to me?" Well, let's say that if I share at the "feeling" level, someone might laugh at my idea or remind me of my past. So what? Move on to someone else.

I also have a little hint. Be a person with eyes of compassion and a warm and friendly handshake. The rewards of intimacy are many. But prepare yourself. Your phone will ring more often, and there will be knocks at your door—occasionally at inconvenient times. The costs of intimacy can be great, but do you really want fear to rule such a potentially fulfilling area of your life?

"IF I DON'T MEET THE EXPECTATIONS OF OTHERS, WHAT WILL HAPPEN TO THEM AND ME?"

Fear 5: Disappointing People

> *When we face how deeply disappointed we are with our relationships, it then becomes possible to recognize the ugliness of what before seemed reasonable. When I realize how badly I want someone to come through for me in a way no one has, then (and not until then) can I see how hard I work either to get what I want or to protect myself from the anguish of more disappointment.*
>
> DR. LARRY CRABB
> *Inside Out*

The headline was not unusual: "San Diego Man Put on House Arrest to Await Trial." But my heart was racing. Breath was short. Eyes brimmed with tears. Terror gripped my heart. The article continued:

A judge Wednesday ordered that a San Diego man charged with attempted murder of a police officer be jailed and then held under house arrest until trial.

Michael Jensen, 37, will wear an electronic monitoring bracelet in his home. . . . The bracelet will allow law enforcement officials to keep track of Jensen, who allegedly shot at his wife and two sheriff's deputies during a domestic dispute at the home on Wednesday, March 4.

. . . Judge Anthony J. Markham said that according to a report, Jensen "shot up everything in the house that reminded him of his wife." . . . One bullet apparently went right over a sheriff's head and hit a squad car. . . .

The Jensens had been seeing a counselor, and their marital problems "came to a head." . . . On the night of the domestic dispute, Megan Jensen left the home and called the sheriff. . . . A standoff began at 7:45 p.m., when Jensen allegedly fired shots from a scope-equipped rifle at his wife and sheriff's deputies. . . .

Jensen held sheriff's deputies at bay and kept his neighbors away from their homes almost three hours . . . [before he] surrendered to about 30 Special Operations Officers [and] was taken to a mental health center.[1]

As I viewed the videotape on the local news that night, it was my sister's face that appeared on the screen. The paralyzing fear that accompanied a phone call on the fateful night of March 4 returned to imprison me. My own sister a victim of domestic violence? How could she have stayed married to an abusive man for nineteen years? What about her ten-year-old son—my nephew!

My thoughts came like water over a dam, filled with anger and rage and guilt for not being more involved in her life—guilt for not being there to "save" her from this situation. From that man. From the humiliation and public embarrassment. Then came the reality of the oppressive fear that consumed me — fear for her life!

This article was not just one more case of spousal abuse. This was my sister, my family member, my flesh and blood — and all the prayer in the world could not quiet my heart.

↳ WHY DO WOMEN PUT UP WITH SO MUCH?

All of us have an indescribable desire for love. We spend much of our lives trying to make relationships work so we can fill the vacuum inside our souls. For most of us, no punishment could be worse than being abandoned by someone to whom we have given our love, loyalty, and commitment.

But this problem goes far beyond the personal feeling of rejection we might experience. Our gripping fear is that significant other people in our lives will know we failed at the one thing Christian women are supposed to be good at — making relationships work. Especially marriage and family relationships!

Most of us would prefer to live with personal pain, emotional deprivation, and spiritual paralysis rather than risk the possibility of disappointing people who we think expect us to be models of Christian womanhood. Sometimes we choose sick marriages, plastic family reunions, and phony church fellowship instead of admitting we have a problem and asking somebody for help. Some of us have functioned at this level for so long, we think it's normal.

↳ KEY QUESTIONS THAT DEMAND
PERSONAL INTROSPECTION

Answer the following questions as honestly as you can:

- In one or more of your closest relationships, do you always give more than you receive?

- Are you fearful of arousing someone's anger if you don't perform certain tasks to his or her liking?
- Do you "cover the tracks" for others you are close to by making excuses, justifying what they haven't done, doing work for them, or even lying to make them look better?
- Do you have trouble communicating in an open, honest, and appropriately confrontational manner with a certain person in your life?
- Do you find yourself "giving in" or "giving up" in order to keep peace in a relationship?
- Do the emotional mood swings of another person drastically affect your personal planning and emotional well-being?
- Do you find yourself constantly "fixing things" so someone else is in a good mood or behaves in a civil manner?

If you answered yes to more than half of these questions, this chapter is for you. The fear of disappointing people is rooted in the fear of abandonment. Most of us struggle with this problem at some level throughout our lifetime.

UNDERSTANDING THE BUZZ WORDS

A few years ago some new words started cropping up in informal conversations everywhere. People in and out of professional counseling services were using terms like *dysfunctional, codependency,* and *enabler.* There were also special initials that the "in" crowd referred to. I remember feeling totally ignorant in a gathering of my peers when someone referred to an ACA group; I had no idea she was talking about "Adult Children of Alcoholics."

Since then, my basic understanding has extended to include at least an elementary knowledge of these terms, and the more I learn, the more interesting the words have become. The three specific buzzwords mentioned above play vital roles in the lives of all of us who are afraid of disappointing people.

DYSFUNCTIONAL

How dysfunctional is *your* family? The names in the following scenarios may be different, but are the people the same?

- Have you ever participated in a family reunion, looked over at weird Uncle Harry and negative Cousin Ethel, and wondered if *all* of the strange people are in *your* family?
- Have you ever attended a family dinner and heard your father/mother argue with your aunt/uncle/grandmother/grandfather for two hours of the three hours they were together? Do you wonder why they choose to get together, because this *always* happens?
- After a perfectly miserable time with relatives, has your mother tried to convince you that all families have a few people who don't get along, but overall it was wonderful reunion?
- Do you or the people in your home blame others for the family tensions with words like, "If only he hadn't said that . . . " or "I wouldn't yell at her if she . . . " or "I can't be responsible for the way I am . . . "?
- Do you prefer being alone to spending time with a family like the one you're in?
- In desperation have you ever given in to an angry outburst directed toward the stupidity of the family members around you?

So what does it mean to be in a "dysfunctional" family? Curt Grayson and Jan Johnson, in a book titled *Creating a Safe Place,* tell us that some people look at the destructive tendencies of dysfunctionality and think it's a fancy name for sin. But that's not true! "Dysfunctionality is not sin; it's a by-product of sin. It's the handicap of an inability to relate to God and others because we were nurtured improperly as children."[2]

During his early years of ministry my father pastored a little country church. This church had some members who were vibrant, effective, growing Christian men and women. It also had some very odd, obstreperous people in attendance. At times I looked forward to leaving for college and getting on with my life so I could go to a church with more "normal" people than we seemed to have in our town.

The day finally came. I grew up and visited several other churches. My husband and I became active in the "perfect" local church. Then one day we faced a milestone in our maturity: *All churches have a few strange people.* As we looked at our families and talked to our friends, we realized, *All families have a few unconventional relatives.* It was somewhat comforting to know, *All of us struggle with dysfunctional people!* Not all of the strange people are in my family or in my church! Some of the dysfunctional people are in *your* family and in *your* church! And the final revelation? *Sometimes I'm the dysfunctional person other people are dealing with!*

When the dysfunctional people we struggle with are in our church or workplaces, we can sometimes hold them at arm's length and make them someone else's problem, but when they're relatives or close friends, it's often a far different story. Because we long so desperately to "help" those we love and because our own successful image is strongly tied to those we are close to, codependency is often triggered.

CODEPENDENCY

Nancy Groom, in her book *From Bondage to Bonding,* defined this word as follows:

> Codependency is a self-focused way of life in which a person blind
> to his or her true self continually reacts to others—being con-
> trolled by and seeking to control their behavior, attitudes, and/or

opinions, resulting in spiritual sterility, loss of authenticity, and absence of intimacy.[3]

Experts in the addiction-recovery field find this word very difficult to define because at one time or another *all* of us have dealt with some level of codependency. Codependents feel controlled by someone else much of the time, regularly adjusting their behavior to keep the status quo in relationships—even those that are abusive and demeaning.

Groom wrote,

> Think of a relationship continuum with healthy mutual inter-dependence at one end and debilitating codependency at the other. We all fall somewhere in between . . . [but] the longer a person pursues codependent strategies for dealing with life, the more codependent he or she becomes. Eventually those strategies become an addictive way of life—a person's primary and compulsive method for relating to self and others.[4]

ENABLER

This role is often played by the spouse, parent, or loyal friend of a dysfunctional person, and it overlaps with codependency. The enabler becomes the "shield" for the alcoholic, workaholic, drug abuser, rageaholic, or depressed person. (After all, we still want this person to "look good" in front of our friends, coworkers, and relatives!) Authors Katherine Ketcham and Ginny Gustafson describe the enabler:

> The chief protector, hiding the Dependent's mistakes, covering up, lying, and making excuses for his behavior. The Enabler acts

out of a sincere sense of love and loyalty, is motivated by fear of the consequences of the Dependent's behavior ("If I don't lie for him, he'll lose his job," "If I don't take care of him, he'll die,"). . . . As the Enabler tries harder and harder to make things right and as things get worse and worse, she suffers from growing self-doubt, self-hatred, guilt, anger, and fear.[5]

✍ MEGAN'S STORY

Megan was raised in the same home I grew up in. Because we loved our parents and wanted to make them proud of us, we were very careful not to do anything that would put a question mark over the validity of their ministry. Because Mom and Dad were visible Christian leaders in our town, the thought of disappointing them by doing something publicly embarrassing was unthinkable!

When Megan met Michael, sparks flew. He was a flamboyant, flashy Italian who enjoyed living on the wild side. Mom and Dad were concerned about his religious upbringing, which was very different from our conservative evangelical training, but when Michael realized an important step in his relationship with Megan's father was to "pray the prayer" and invite Christ into his life, he quickly obliged. Within a few months the wedding date was set.

Michael and Megan tied the knot in lavish celebration of what appeared to represent the portrait of an ideal marriage. Soon after the wedding, they moved to San Diego — far from the watchful eyes of Mom and Dad, and far from the potential of casting a negative shadow over the ministry.

In the beginning they were happy. Michael was possessive in his love, and Megan was young enough to enjoy being his "private obsession." But after a while, his heavy domination became a burden to her. Megan had to answer twenty questions after she returned from short shopping trips. She had no freedom to pursue personal friendships apart from Michael's total involvement in the relationships.

Megan gave birth to a baby boy and began staying at home to run Michael's construction business from an in-house office. She became the bookkeeper, the office and personnel manager, and the charming voice that booked future business over the phone. Michael's outrageous emotional ups and downs and his lack of interest in the details and paperwork of self-employment left Megan in charge of "making Michael look good"—to the clients, the IRS, the relatives, the neighbors, and even to his young son.

When Michael was in a good mood, no one could be more fun. But when he was raging mad or feeling threatened or overwhelmed with financial problems, he was in a frenzy. He had developed a library of pornographic material and began insisting that Megan live up to the models of perfection on his favorite videos. She would be summoned to the bedroom on a moment's notice—even when guests were in the house. At one point Michael stated, "I only feel safe when I'm inside of you." Megan was always quick to make "appropriate" excuses for his demanding and bizarre behavior.

His sessions of rage started to come more frequently. When he was upset, he destroyed property—expensive personal property. The next day he would apologize and try to "fix" his mistakes by buying new things.

As the financial crunch hit, Megan acquired her credentials for selling real estate and joined a prestigious firm in the city. Soon she had a large car, a cell phone, important appointments, and her own growing income. Megan no longer had the time and energy she once possessed to cover all of Michael's tracks. But she tried.

When her parents or sisters phoned, she hid the truth from them, indicating life with Michael was blissfully happy. She even began using her own income to cover debt incurred by Michael's wild spending sprees. Megan's codependency had brought her to a place of enabling Michael to continue in his self-destructive mode. And she was almost killed in the process.

13 WHAT CAUSES CODEPENDENCY?

How do we wind up with this problem of codependence? Most of us long to be loving women who reach out to the needs of family members and friends in healthy, authentic, and appropriately intimate ways. How does something that sounds so correct become distorted and destructive?

Why does the fear of disappointing people play such a major role in our lives? Why do we wind up feeling emotionally bankrupt and spiritually empty? There are many potential trigger points, but some vital causes that women have shared with me are listed below:

FEAR OF DISAPPOINTING GOD

This fear is a natural for Christian women. Most of us have been raised with a strong work ethic, and we believe in the concept of "serving people in love." We believe that giving of ourselves to help others is basic to what Scripture teaches. With our deep desire to have a strong Christian home, we wind up enabling our "less spiritual" spouses or family members to look more "godly" by controlling their behavior, attitudes, and opinions.

This cycle of failure often continues for years without the codependent person realizing she has taken Scripture out of context. When we wind up adding our own flawed interpretations to what the Word of God says, we come up with a distorted view of a biblical concept.

MISUNDERSTANDING SUBMISSION

Christian women know the Bible teaches that the husband is the head of the home, as Christ is the head of the church. The guidelines for a successful and happy marriage are definitely found in Scripture. However, some verses have been lifted from their context to authenticate an erroneous teaching about Christian marriage.

In *Love Is a Choice,* Doctors Hemfelt, Minirth, and Meier explain this false understanding of Scripture:

> In 1 Corinthians 7:4 [we] accept Paul's teaching that the husband
> rules over the wife's body—ignoring the rest of that verse . . . that
> says the wife rules over the husband's body. In that same chapter,
> verse 10, Paul declares that a wife should not separate from her hus-
> band. Yet, how few women are counseled in the rest of that same
> verse— *"but if she does"* . . . Paul left the door open for extreme cases.
>
> The wife is called upon to be subject to her man (Ephesians
> 5:22), but hardly anyone notices that in 5:21 Paul has used
> exactly the same word to call every Christian into similar submis-
> sion to every other. . . . The abusive husband quotes Hebrews
> 12:7, which extols God's disciplining of His faithful, and twists it
> to suggest that the man ought to keep his mature adult wife in
> line in the same way one might discipline a small child, or God
> might discipline an errant saint.[6]

Often, the woman who has been taught that her chief duty is to "stand
by her man" believes that since divorce is unthinkable for the Christian
woman, she should just put up with mental, physical, and sexual abuse. She
fails to fully understand that the same Scripture (1 Corinthians 7:32-37) just
as firmly states that the husband should please his wife.

The doctors quoted earlier state,

> Especially in Christian marriage, denominational interpretation
> and tradition bind the woman to an unholy union of fear and
> pain. Because of her erroneous concept of submission and her
> strong abhorrence of divorce or separation, the Christian wife
> may have little recourse but to take refuge in terrible denial . . .
> [which] is compounded by false guilt.[7]

This woman often hears her husband say, "If you would just submit to me the way the Bible teaches, I wouldn't have to yell at you (or discipline you)." The codependent woman believes that *she* is responsible for his negative actions and attitude. Her self-esteem is so fragile, she quickly accepts the blame for almost anything!

LOST CHILDHOOD

Women who were abused as children easily fall into codependent relationships in their adulthood. They often experience an undercurrent of guilt, which leads them to believe they could have stopped the perpetrators of the abuse if they were smart enough or strong enough. This leads to low self-esteem, which reinforces a cycle of trying to be helpful or good enough to please the powerful people around them. They feel the most self-worth when they are "fixing things" for the alcoholic, workaholic, rageaholic, or drug-addicted person.

The firstborn woman frequently fits into this category as well. If there were several siblings, she may have taken on adult responsibilities at an early age and learned how to "make peace" between arguing family members and "rescue" brothers and sisters from the wrath of a dysfunctional parent. The habits of a lifetime often lead the firstborn woman into becoming an adult enabler, who is so absorbed and enmeshed in the life and conflicts of someone else that she loses her own sense of self in the process.

13 THE DESTRUCTIVE PATH OF FEAR

Life is complicated. I am one of five sisters. All of us were raised under the same roof with the same parents. We had the same theologically sound upbringing, with similar opportunities and challenges, but our lives have taken very different turns.

When the call came on that March evening, announcing that my sister had run from her home as shots were fired in her direction, I was numb. Why would my brother-in-law get a gun from his collection and begin shooting up the house? Why did he "go over the edge" in such a violent way?

Other thoughts consumed my mind. Why did my sister keep her mental and sexual abuse such a secret? Why did she enable him to continue in his destructive path by making calls to appease his creditors? Why did she always make excuses for him when family members visited? When he became raging mad and destroyed expensive personal property, why did she welcome him back into her good graces the next day when he offered his predictable "I'm sorry"?

It's much easier to evaluate codependency from a gallery seat as a spectator than when we are living through it in a dysfunctional family situation. The fear of disappointing people has deep foundations in our past. For a time, the outward characteristics of codependency have the appearance of everything we admire in a caring Christian woman: helping, meeting needs, making peace in the middle of chaos, creating a "good testimony" for the family, keeping people with addictions from making fools of themselves, and protecting children from a dysfunctional parent. The list could go on and on. How could something that looks so "spiritual" become so destructive?

Megan's story has been repeated, with a few variations, in every city in North America. What happened?

Triggering situation: Prior to Megan's whirlwind romance with Michael she had been in love with a man her father had disapproved of. With a deep desire to meet the expectations of her family and to protect her father's ministry from potential controversy, she broke off the relationship, even though the decision brought her deep personal pain.

She married Michael within a year after saying goodbye to her first love. Michael was the fifth child born to an economically deprived family, and he was the only child in the family who was given up for adoption.

Although he was raised by parents who adored him and gave him every benefit money and love could provide, Michael still knew he was the only child abandoned by his birth parents. Thus, his "love tank" was always on empty and the only way he knew how to compensate was to control Megan with an unhealthy, obsessive love.

In the beginning, Michael and Megan had many happy times together. They both enjoyed outdoor sports in sunny California, but a dark cloud came over the marriage as Michael's control began stifling Megan's personhood.

Reactive emotion: Megan began to experience fear on many levels. Michael began destroying property when he was angry. At times, she feared for her own safety and that of her son. On another level she was deeply afraid of hurting the testimony of her mother and father if word of Michael's violence and their marriage problems became widely known. She had recurring fears that *she* might be the person causing Michael's problems. Perhaps if she were a more submissive wife, he wouldn't become so violent.

Had marrying Michael been the worst mistake of her life? Was it *her* fault he went into an angry rage and threw the telephone on the floor, demolishing it in the process? And what about the time he destroyed the television in a spurt of anger? If only she met his needs more completely, he wouldn't buy pornographic magazines and videos. Maybe if she was a better wife, he might be a better man.

Powerlessness: It didn't take long for Megan to feel powerless and betrayed. Earlier, her conservative Christian father had kept her from marrying the man she cared for so deeply. Later, Michael eroded her confidence and made her feel incapable of changing her downward spiral. Finally, she felt betrayed by God.

Rage: After a while, anger began to fester. It didn't take long for Megan's sense of betrayal to turn to rage. She had tried her best to be an obedient daughter and a submissive wife. Did God see what was happening and how miserable she was? Apparently not!

Internal negotiating: During the powerless stage, we tend to get our focus off Christ and on our own crisis and our intense need. After rage sets in, we decide *to do something ourselves*—since the people we may have trusted haven't come through for us. Thus, self-reliance becomes our crutch. Our internal negotiation leads us to take action.

Destructive resolution: When internal negotiating brings on a rigid "I'll do it myself" decision for dealing with fear, we often choose denial, defeat, bitterness, or escape into obsessive/compulsive behaviors. In the beginning, Megan chose *denial*. She had married this man and she was going to make it work. She began convincing herself his emotional fits of rage were the same as any man venting his disapproval. His sexual obsession and outlandish physical demands were sometimes unbearable, but God said she was supposed to give herself to her husband and she did.

In the end Megan chose a "survival mode" through the *escape* called codependency. She became skilled at hiding Michael's mistakes, covering up the aftermath of his violent rage, and making excuses for his behavior. For years, it seemed like the right decision. It made her feel like a "biblically correct" wife; it kept her from embarrassing her parents with a divorced daughter; it kept a raging husband under control much of the time. But her life was spiritually sterile. She had a loss of self-respect, and a total absence of intimacy.

✍ RISKING CHANGE

Redesigning our lives with the benefits of time, maturity, wise counsel, and hindsight is time consuming and costly. People may question our judgment. We may feel unspiritual for changing codependent habits. Family members may feel temporarily displaced.

Our long-term struggle with low self-esteem asserts itself with determination, begging us to accept the blame for making the lives of those around us uncomfortable during the transition to wholeness. Their words reverberate: "You're abandoning us and all of your 'Christian' duties. You are responsible for this chaos!"

The journey to self-respect is full of challenges, questions, second thoughts, and hope for a better future. As you begin to release the fear of disappointing people, remember:

- The controlling person in your life did not take a look in your direction and decide to make you miserable. He or she is responding out of dysfunction: an inability to relate to God and others, perhaps because of improper nurturing as a child. *Can you forgive him or her for that?*

- We are all flawed human beings. If you have identified yourself as an enabler, you hurt the person you want to help by allowing this codependency to continue. *Are you willing to pick up a phone and find out where you can get Christian counseling?*

- God's plan for marriage is not a dictatorship. The reference to the husband being the head of the home as Christ is the head of the church is often misinterpreted. The day-to-day outworking of that level of love means serving each other sacrificially, with *mutual respect and honor.* The husband who treats his wife like a wayward child or a disobedient servant in the name of "biblical submission" is misunderstanding or misinterpreting Scripture. *Are you willing to appropriately confront your husband if you are being treated like a doormat?* (A similar scenario could be present in any relationship where there is an imbalance of power.)

- God's ideal is for unbroken, intimate fellowship in our significant relationships. But we live in a fallen world where people make sinful choices. When problems arise, every effort should be made to bring about biblical reconciliation; however, if we allow our fear of disappointing people to keep us from confronting serious codependency issues, we are making a mistake. When these serious concerns are dealt with, there is the potential of a relationship that exceeds our expectations. But sometimes, if both parties are not willing to face their responsiblity for discord, ending the relationship becomes necessary. *Has your fear of disappointing people kept you from taking a biblical step toward confronting an unhealthy relationship in your life?*

⚂ POSTSCRIPT

Megan practiced "tough love" when Michael refused to continue with counseling over their marriage problems and codependency issues. She made arrangements for a separation, which triggered Michael's violent response. Megan is now living in another state, and her marriage ended in divorce.

Megan's story does not have a fairy-tale ending, but she has made some important faith-filled decisions and she no longer lives in fear for her life. She knows that confronting her husband about past abuses was a godly decision. She has realized she is not responsible for the wrong choices of her husband. She knows Mom and Dad will still be dynamic Christian leaders even though they have a divorced daughter.

Many years have passed since Megan's father rejected her first love. All of us mature in our spiritual understanding and application of biblical principles over time, and my dad had the wisdom to write a letter of apology to Megan. He told her he had come to realize he was very wrong and should not have interfered in her relationship with this man so many years ago. There has been some precious healing in our family.

The emptiness inside of Megan is in the process of being filled. She has grieved for her losses, which are many. She no longer needs to hide behind self-protective pretense. She is learning the meaning of God's empowering grace and is finding help beyond herself. Her life is honest and authentic— and she is learning how to develop intimate relationships based on mutual trust and nonpossessive love. Megan is a courageous woman. You can be, too.

"WHAT IF THE PEOPLE I'VE GIVEN MY LOVE TO LEAVE ME OR BETRAY ME?"

Fear 6: Being Rejected

Few things make us more aware of our need for the Lord than rejection. The only final cure for the frowning face of rejection is His smiling face of love and acceptance. And the more we wait for Him, the less we'll wait in fear of future rejection.

DR. LLOYD OGILVIE
12 Steps to Living Without Fear

The letter had an out-of-state address. I opened the handwritten note and began to read:

My husband left me three years ago to live as a homosexual. . . . He admitted he came back to me for the kids. . . . Can you give me any advice on how to live with a totally self-centered man?

I'm expected to be perfect—right down to keeping a flawlessly tidy laundry room (is there such a thing?), yet he denies me sexually and will not try to see our relationship in a positive light. . . . I have two children who love their dad, but my husband doesn't love me. I am going through a dark emotional time. I don't want to be his maid or prostitute . . . he said he loved me before he married me, but he betrayed me on our first anniversary.

As I continued reading the lengthy account of Nancy's rejection, I realized how many other women face the same emotion, even when the triggering situation is different.

- A flight attendant wrote: "I have been going through a 'gray period' for quite a long time, which has become even blacker lately. I keep making choices in my life that I think are 'right,' but they continuously leave me alone and unhappy. . . . I appear superficially happy, but I'm sad inside most of the time."

- An executive woman recounted her story: "I dated a man for two years who said he cared deeply for me. I was a virgin who always planned to 'save myself' for the one man I would marry. This man convinced me he had several business problems during our two-year relationship and kept putting off setting a wedding date. I finally 'gave myself' to him physically, thinking it would be a short time before we were married anyway. He made promises, but never followed through. I finally realized he *never* planned to marry me. He was enjoying the single life too much. I feel angry, hurt, betrayed, and robbed!"

- A young mother voiced her fear: "When I married Mark, I trusted him completely. We had dedicated our lives to the Lord and fully expected to go into full-time Christian ministry. Over a period of months following our marriage, I began to realize that my husband was hopelessly addicted to marijuana. He knew I wouldn't approve, so he hid his habit, used money needed for our bills to support his addiction, and then began lying to me.

"After he 'came clean' two years ago, I caught him again. You can imagine how I felt when the truth came out—for the second time! We have two small children who need their father to be a positive role model. I am angry—even bitter, wondering how on earth I am ever going to respect this person. . . . I'm having a hard time dealing with my feelings toward him. I feel like he has betrayed my love and our future in ministry for his habit."

■ A single female missionary in Europe voiced her anguish: "I work among people who have a spirit of self-sufficiency. On my mission field people seem to feel that they have everything they need, so they don't require God. No matter how hard I work there are very few visible results to report to my supporting churches when I'm home on furlough.

"I have been devastated by a letter from my mission requesting that I submit my resignation. I was told that my home church had questions about the degree of effectiveness of my last term of ministry. I have given the best years of my life to the Lord through this mission, and I am being totally rejected by the ministry I love. I feel betrayed and angry!"

■ A woman in her sixties wrote: "Last spring my husband of forty-one years left me when I discovered he had been involved in a long-term affair with a woman in our church. He also left his position of leadership in our denomination. He says he plans to divorce me, marry this woman, and start a church for 'hurting people.'

"I am bitter and confused. I cry all the time. I used to be happy, but I can barely function anymore. I don't see how God can get any glory through the things that have happened to me. I have been rejected by my husband—and now I feel rejected by my church. I have never needed help more, but instead of reaching out to me, the people in my denomination seem to want me to go away—along with the embarrassment this whole incident has caused in our community."

⚕ WHAT IS THE FEAR OF ABANDONMENT?

Lonely. Abandoned. Misunderstood. Rejected. Betrayed. How many times have you and I needed more than one of those words to describe what we're feeling?

When we have poured our energy, passion, and time into the lives of people, we instinctively expect something in return. Are those expectations wrong? Why do friends consistently let us down? Why are we lonely in the middle of a crowd? How can someone we trust completely betray us? Why would anyone reject a genuine offer of love?

When we are abandoned, someone deserts us. Whether the experience is an emotional or a physical desertion, the experience of being "cast off" is the same. We are unwanted. Unfrequented. Undesired. The fear of abandonment is closely linked to the fear of rejection. When we believe we might be "thrown away as worthless" by someone we desired to have a relationship with, the fear can be paralyzing.

One woman described her fear of abandonment in this way:

It is the dread of not being wanted. I am never sure the people who are displaying love toward me are doing it because they really want to. Maybe they feel obligated. It's the fear of being an imposition upon someone. Rooted deeply in false guilt, it shows up in a sense of insecurity when I'm with others.

The fear of abandonment often binds women to the compulsive behavior of clutching at people so closely they feel strangled. When we believe that letting go of someone means we will be left behind, we are in bondage to fear. This fear inhibits intimacy and causes deep pain. One pastor states, "The fear of rejection not only keeps us from deep relationships, it often robs us of courage. We become solicitous and compliant. Eventually like a chameleon we try to blend into the background of other people's values and attitudes."[1]

Abandonment issues can be hidden deeply and covered up in many subtle disguises. Think about the people you care about the most or the people you would like to develop a closer relationship with. Do you ever entertain the following thoughts?

- If I tell you the truth about my past, you will push me away.
- If I'm vulnerable with you, I could be humiliated.
- I have been betrayed by someone in the past, and it won't happen to me again.
- If I don't change my appearance, you will think I'm fat and unattractive, and you might reject me.
- I feel threatened when you develop a close friendship with someone else.
- I feel unworthy of your love.
- I know you have many important things to do and many influential people in your life, so you probably don't really want to develop a friendship with someone like me.
- The people I've trusted the most in the past have let me down. I wonder when you will abandon me.
- I will work hard to avoid disappointing you, because if you reject me, I will have nobody.

✍ WHAT CAUSES WOMEN TO FEAR REJECTION?

LONELINESS

The fear of rejection is often precipitated by loneliness. In an article titled "All Alone: The New Loneliness of American Women," Margery Rosen says loneliness is triggered when our need for an intimate, caring relationship goes unmet. She quotes psychologist Anne Peplau, who said, "At any given time, at least ten percent of the population feels lonely."[2]

According to Robert S. Weiss, Ph.D., a research professor at the University of Massachusetts in Boston and a pioneer in loneliness research, there are actually two types of loneliness: emotional and social.

> We *feel* emotionally lonely when we aren't sharing our life with . . . an attachment figure. . . . People who suffer this form of loneliness often display real physical symptoms—an intense restlessness that makes it difficult to concentrate, a heaviness in the chest.
>
> But while some women—especially those who live alone— have always felt emotionally lonely, now they are increasingly susceptible to what Weiss calls social loneliness. "People who are socially lonely feel marginal." They tend to blame themselves for their isolation. "They may harbor a feeling that people don't like them—a sense that everyone was invited to the party but them."[3]

PAST ISSUES

Women who were victims of abuse often feel abandoned by the adult who overlooked obvious evidence of their exploitation and did nothing to help. One woman wrote, "My mother would have had to be blind to be unaware of my father's sexual relationship with me. Why didn't she do something to protect me from that sickening animal? I was only eight years old when it started."

Those who felt abandoned as children often carry those feelings into adulthood. Rejection can be real or imagined, but this genuine emotion often leads to a sense of abandonment. Sherrie writes,

> As an adopted child, I was never sure that I was wanted, even
> though I was told I was. My parents had never worked through
> their own grief about having been childless, and I translated their
> subtle sadness to mean they were disappointed in me. So I
> worked hard to make them proud of me, because if I disap-
> pointed them, they might reject me, and then I would have no
> one in this world. . . . Out of a fear of abandonment, I had to pre-
> tend to be somebody "special." This produced a drivenness in my
> lifestyle from childhood.

BETRAYAL

Looking back at the excerpts from letters that were printed at the beginning of this chapter, it's easy to see why betrayal triggers the fear of rejection:

- The homosexual husband who kept his secret until the first anniversary
- The flight attendant who felt betrayed by a fallen world that promised fulfillment
- The executive who was betrayed by the man she believed would marry her
- The young mother who was betrayed by the addiction of her husband
- The missionary betrayed by her Christian financial and prayer supporters
- The older woman betrayed by her husband, his lover, and the church congregation

Max Lucado reminds us of the sting of betrayal:

> *Betray.* The word is an eighth of an inch above *betroth* in the dic-
> tionary, but a world from "betroth" in life. It's a weapon found
> only in the hands of one you love. Your enemy has no such tool,
> for only a friend can betray. Betrayal is mutiny. It's a violation of
> trust, an inside job. . . . You look to your friends and your friends
> don't look back. You look to the system for justice—the system
> looks to you as a scapegoat.[4]

Betrayal's worst insult is the pilfering of innocence. Once we have felt
the barb, endured the mockery, and experienced the insult, our relationships
are never the same again. Betrayal bleeds the heart of its ability to trust.
Insecurity replaces confidence. Hesitancy displaces certainty. Skepticism
uproots faith. The fear of rejection erases acceptance.

SPIRITUAL VOID

An intriguing story is recorded in 1 Kings 17. It had been fifty years since
Israel was at the pinnacle of spiritual success under David and Solomon.
Now Ahab was king. Jezebel was his wife. This was more than a marriage—
it was an evil alliance. Under this diabolical leadership, Israel was plunged
into the appalling rituals and sexual orgies of Baal and Ashteroth, pagan
deities dedicated to violence and sexual perversion.

At this crucial time in Israel's history Elijah was selected to be God's
public speaker for his generation. God's change agent. But when the script
for his first talk came from God, it was one line long and it was the last time
Elijah was allowed to speak publicly for about three and a half years! "As
surely as GOD lives, the God of Israel before whom I stand in obedient service, the next years are going to see a total drought—not a drop of dew or
rain unless I say otherwise" (1 Kings 17:1).

Immediately after God opened a major door of ministry for Elijah, he got new instructions: "GOD then told Elijah, *Get out of here, and fast. Head east and hide out at the Kerith Ravine. . . . You can drink fresh water from the brook; I've ordered the ravens to feed you. . . .* Elijah obeyed GOD's orders. . . ." But after a while, "the brook dried up" (summary of 1 Kings 17:2-7).

Did you get that? After what appeared to be a big-time opportunity for powerful and visible ministry, God sent Elijah to the brook—but it dried up. It shut down. It quit meeting his needs. It left him thirsty.

Those words jump off the page as I think about my own relationship with God. When was the last time in my life "the brook dried up"? Dry brooks take many forms:

- The opportunity for ministry or work that was going to bring me fulfillment didn't.
- The promised job never came through.
- The baby I asked God for has not been conceived.
- The friend who had cancer was not healed, in spite of my fervent prayers.
- The child I nurtured is on drugs.
- The friend who led me to Jesus contracted the HIV virus from her husband.
- The teenage daughter I love is pregnant.
- The pastor I trusted left his wife.
- The intimacy I long for with God is elusive.

When the brook dries up, dreams are shattered. Hopes are dashed. God seems far away. We feel abandoned by people we were hoping would satisfy our needs. But more than that, we feel rejected by a God who should have intervened in our situation. The One who is Living Water and says He loves us and wants to meet our needs has allowed the brook to dry up.

⅓ SHERRIE'S GREATEST FEAR

Sherrie was released for adoption at ten days of age. As an adopted child, she wanted to please her parents. She had perceived their sadness regarding infertility. So Sherrie tried hard to be "good enough" to please them and take away their pain.

She was convinced her mother and father's grief over not being able to conceive a child meant they were very disappointed in the little girl they adopted. Sherrie's fear of rejection followed her. When she became pregnant out of wedlock, she took the fear of abandonment into marriage. The question always haunted her: Did Bob marry me because he really wanted to, or because he was stuck with me? Her life became consumed with the need to be "special" enough to keep him from being disappointed in her—and abandoning her. She became a driven wife and mother.

During twenty-seven years of homemaking and motherhood she tried to be the perfect hostess, laundress, gourmet cook, maid, and interior decorator. As she contemplated returning to college, she wondered, Would my husband abandon me if I no longer did these tasks so well? It was hard for Sherrie to accept Bob's total acceptance and unconditional love.

Sherrie's adoptive parents both passed away, and she had a growing desire to find the answers to the abandonment issues that left her feeling powerless and hurt. After a long search, Sherrie's birth mother was located. An emotional phone call was made and within ten days, Sherrie and her husband were on a 727 headed for Seattle, Washington.

Initially, the reunion was a fairy-tale experience. Sherrie's birth mother greeted her with every imaginable sign of acceptance: a bouquet of her favorite flowers in the hotel suite, a diamond-studded pin from Tiffany's, and a sign over the front door of the family home that read, "WELCOME TO YOUR FAMILY."

Within ten days, Sherrie went from being an only child, with both parents dead, to being a sister and a daughter. During the visit her birth mother's words were tender as she looked at Sherrie and spoke softly, "When I look at your sweet face, I know you're mine." With sensitivity she continued, "You are my angel. I love you."

As the next few days progressed, Sherrie felt the Master Healer doing a deep work within her soul, healing wounds of the past. It was so much fun discovering all the similarities: same voice, same facial features, same tastes and talents. Every discovery was a gift, a piece of the puzzle that had been missing all of Sherrie's life.

But as the week progressed, Sherrie's birth mother began to get in touch with her pain—pain from the past that had never been resolved. Her pain threw her totally out of control. Her choices were clear: she could face the pain of the past and get help, or put Sherrie out of her life and regain the control that provided a false sense of security. And without warning, she closed the door on any future relationship with her daughter. As Sherrie boarded the plane to return home, she knew her mother was saying goodbye.

HOW DID THE CHAIN REACTION WORK?

Triggering event: Sherrie's cycle of fear was triggered by the knowledge that her birth mother had "given her up" for adoption at ten days of age. She knew nothing of her nationality, her family's medical history, and very little about why she had been released for adoption by her family of origin.

Reactive emotion: Sherrie's fear of rejection started in childhood when she sensed her parents' longing to conceive a child. She was convinced that meant they were displeased with her and might abandon her too.

Powerlessness: As a child with no place to go and no one to talk to about her fear, Sherrie was powerless to change her circumstances or deal with her fear of rejection in a constructive manner.

Rage: Sometimes we think of rage as a violent show of emotion—and it can be. But for Sherrie, the anger was inside. Why had she been given away? Why was she placed with a family that wanted a biological child? On the surface Sherrie was a model child. But her internal rage boiled with unanswered questions.

Internal negotiating: Sherrie needed to find a way to "fix" her problem. It's at this point when each of us has a choice. We can choose the path of self-reliance and say, "I'll take care of the problem myself." Or we can choose the path of God-reliance and focus on a constructive course of action.

Escape: It didn't take Sherrie long at all to escape into a lifelong pattern of perfectionism, first as an adopted daughter who tried to be "good enough" to please her parents. As a young, pregnant newlywed, she tried to be "perfect enough" to please her husband. For twenty-seven years the pattern continued—with a lot of happiness mingled in with the compulsive perfectionism. During the first years of marriage, two beautiful daughters were born, and Sherrie tried to make a warm, open, and loving home for Bob and the girls.

13 THE TURNING POINT

A major turning point for Sherrie came with the gut-wrenching rejection from the birth mother she had longed to know. When we face our fears and allow our pain, insecurities, and anger to bring us to our knees, we can reach a God-honoring resolution.

Sorrow: Sherrie had spent years in a self-destructive escape pattern of perfectionism as she sought to cover up her feelings of betrayal, powerlessness, hurt, and rejection. Her mother's cold goodbye at the airport brought Sherrie deep pain.

Sometimes we forget that it's okay with God if we feel the sadness profoundly. We live in a world of imperfection, broken relationships, and unresolved conflict.

Brokenness: We take a major step when we come to the place of admitting how needy we really are.

Sherrie describes the sorrow that led her to brokenness in this way:

> I was in intense pain. I felt the anguish of being rejected. I felt so in touch with the little girl inside of me who was never sure she was wanted. I felt used. I felt disposable and discarded. I called my friend and when she arrived, I began sobbing and shaking uncontrollably.

The Sherrie of former days would have buried her pain by escaping into perfectionism. She would have figured out a way to be "good enough" so her mother would accept her once again. Instead, she let go of self-reliance and, with a humble heart, asked for help.

Surrender: People who control their lives by perfectionism often find letting go very difficult. Sherrie surrendered her desires to God. She asked Him to remove the false guilt she had carried for years. She quit blaming her adoptive parents and her birth mother for her problems. As Sherrie focused on Him, Christ made His presence very real to her through Isaiah 49:15—"Can a mother forget the infant at her breast, walk away from the baby she bore? But even if mothers forget, I'd never forget you—never."

Faith-filled decision: Surrender always leads to a supernatural strength that enables us to make God-honoring, faith-filled decisions. Instead of constantly longing for her family of origin, Sherrie is finding deep fulfillment with her brothers and sisters in the body of Christ. She is leaning on them during times of need, instead of trying to be good enough to earn acceptance. She made the decision to go back to school and earned her bachelor's degree in journalism. Taking a risk, she recently submitted an article to a well-known Christian periodical, and it was accepted!

Sherrie is still a gourmet cook and entertains her guests with a touch of class, but she is no longer a slave to her home. Life with her husband is happier and more balanced. Bob and Sherrie support each other in being whole, complete individuals.

∕ɜ LESSONS FROM ELIJAH

Elijah must have felt abandoned. First, by God as he waited patiently for new instructions. Then came total rejection by Jezebel. Four hundred and fifty prophets of Baal had been destroyed. She was not a happy camper! Remember the note she sent him after the big scene on Mount Carmel?

> Dear Elijah,
>> You are dead meat.
>> Love, Jezebel
>> (Loose paraphrase of 1 Kings 19:2; to get the whole story read 1 Kings 17-19.)

When Elijah faced his worst fear, he chose a destructive resolution for his problem—defeat!

> He ran for dear life . . . and then went on into the desert another day's journey. He came to a lone broom bush and collapsed in its shade, wanting in the worst way to be done with it all—to just die: *"Enough of this, GOD! Take my life—I'm ready to join my ancestors in the grave!"* (1 Kings 19:3-4)

But the end of the story reminds us that it is never too late to resolve our fear in a God-honoring way. God sent an angel to minister to Elijah.

Then the word of the Lord came—but not in an expected way. One would think He would come dramatically—in the wind, the earthquake, or the fire. But not so. He came in a gentle whisper.

> Today, because we have the completed Word of God readily available to us any time of the day or night, we have an advantage. So—the next time you fear rejection and you feel abandoned, remember, "We do not have to wait for the Lord to come to us, for He has never left us. What we are to wait for is the complete fullness of His healing. The only way that this can be speeded up is to trust Him with our hurts sooner."[5]

As we experience the deep *sorrow* of rejection and abandonment, our *brokenness* before God leads to a *surrender* of our stubborn, self-reliant will and paves the road for future *faith-filled decisions* that bring healing, acceptance, and nonpossessive love.

A GLANCE AT GETHSEMANE

Those of us who fear rejection and have experienced abandonment need only look back at the garden where Jesus spent His final precrucifixion hours to forever stamp the truth in our hearts: *He knows what abandonment feels like. He knew the ultimate rejection.*

Calvin Miller reminds us of that night:

> The life in question was His own. He needed friends to watch with Him and support Him as He faced death. He reached. Oh, how He reached! But His stretching, hungering touch went unfulfilled. There was but one gift He desired—to see His friends

stand by Him as He carried out His faithful purpose.

In Gethsemane, Christ found Himself abandoned—not because His friends were gone, but because they took His giant needs too casually. . . . They never wanted Him to be alone, but His need escaped them as they focused on themselves.

Here and there we stumble blind in grief through our Gethsemanes and find the ground already stained with His blood. In our Gethsemanes there's an unseen plaque on every twisted tree, "Jesus was here." He is still here, and we can bear with our Good Fridays if we let our Thursdays call to mind the glorious solitude of Him who conquered loneliness.[6]

We are not alone
   . . . when our brook dries up,
   . . . when our friends and family abandon us,
   . . . when today's cross blinds us to tomorrow's opportunities.

This is my prayer:

God, in the middle of my Gethsemanes help me to remember that You conquered loneliness. You know what my agonizing pain feels like. The total rejection. The "Judas kiss." The abandonment. Change my focus from lonely Gesthemane to Easter Sunday morning.

"IF I REMEMBER AND REVEAL WHAT HAPPENED TO ME, WILL THE PAIN BE INSURMOUNTABLE?"

Fear 7: Facing My Past

> *You have been damaged. But you have great hope. The mercy of God does not eradicate the damage, at least not in this life, but it soothes the soul and draws it forward to a hope that purifies and sets free. Allow the pain of the past and the travail of the change process to create fresh new life in you and to serve as a bridge over which another victim may walk from death to life.*
>
> DR. DAN ALLENDER
> *The Wounded Heart*

As a young child, I had a strictly enforced bedtime. But I was so terrified by the darkness that my mother installed a night light. That minuscule stream of light provided just enough illumination for me to use my hands to form all kinds of amusing shadows on the wall. I remember my excitement when I first learned how to form the image of Mickey Mouse. Then I went on to create a variety of unique animal shapes.

However, when my experimental shadows produced monster images instead of familiar facsimiles of delightful creatures, my fears resurfaced. Knowing my father would be angry if I was a "fraidy cat," I developed a series of reassuring phrases I could call out. Each response demanded an answer from a parent—and when I heard the return call, I knew I was safe from the shadow monsters.

Some of my favorite nighttime proclamations were:

- "See you in the morning!"
- "Hugs and kisses . . . sweet dreams too!"
- "I love you."
- "Sleep tight . . . don't let the bedbugs bite."

SHADOW MONSTERS FROM THE PAST

Each of us has a set of our own "shadow monsters." This time, however, we're not playing a child's game. We are remembering a vivid image from our personal history.

Our fears related to past events loom over us at unexpected times. They crowd out present happiness and cast a dark cloud over future success. As time erodes the exact memory of key events and people that produced our pain, hurt, or disillusionment, the shadow gets larger, and the potential for shame, guilt, anger, and hatred is enhanced.

Some of the shadow monsters faced by women I have talked to include the following:

- "I despise my father for leaving my mother, my two sisters, and me to marry his secretary."

- "I was abused by a church that took advantage of my eagerness to serve the Lord by giving me so many responsibilities and obligations that I nearly had a nervous breakdown."

- "When I was twelve years old my father began sexually molesting me. The need for my father's love and affection was so great that I could not stop him or tell anyone about the problem. My mother knew, but she was a victim of the fear of abandonment, so she looked the other way. After several years the incest ended, but the shame and guilt continued.

  "When I married, I never told my husband. I didn't want him to hate my father. I knew it would destroy the image he had of our 'perfect family.' I built a wall around myself, giving the outward appearance of a vibrant and confident Christian, while frustration and anger grew within me. My rage was vented on my children—and I hated myself for it!"

- "My parents paid for my brother's university education because he would be the 'breadwinner' in his future home. Even though my academic record was much better than my brother's, I wasn't encouraged to go to college. I resent my parents to this day for treating me like an inferior human being because I am a female."

- "I aborted my first baby when I was eighteen years old. I was not in love with the father of the child. I was too young and immature for single parenting, and an abortion counselor convinced me that I was getting rid of excess 'tissue' and an unnecessary responsibility by making the best decision for my future. I now struggle with severe guilt over the life I took."

- "I had an affair with my best friend's husband several years ago.

Even though the physical intimacy with this man ended quickly, my 'emotional affair' with him continued for two years. I'm afraid of getting found out—but I'm even more afraid of facing my own image in the mirror every morning."

- "I stole money from my boss when funds were tight at home a couple of years ago. He's a very successful, highly motivated employer who has done everything to make my job mentally stimulating and personally challenging. I feel tremendous guilt for having taken advantage of someone who has treated me with such respect."

- "Someone else received the promotion that should have been given to me. I have invested my loyalty and the best years of my life in this company and have gotten *nothing* in return! I am hurt, angry, and resentful."

13 THE FEAR OF TRUTH

Whether through victimization or our own behavior, many of us have been held in the grip of our fearful "shadow monsters" for too many years. Some of us spend a lifetime trying to work hard enough and smile long enough to convince ourselves and other people that we're okay. But we're always looking over our shoulder, remembering an event from yesterday or recounting the details of a failed relationship or reliving the horror of abuse—and we are running from the truth.

We believe that if we gave ourselves permission and time to face our past, we would be overwhelmed by shame and guilt—and more anger. Rather than exploring the feelings those memories reveal, it's easier to bury our fears in denial, defeat, bitterness, or a wide variety of escapes. And the cycle of fear continues.

13 AN UNWANTED CHILD

My mother-in-law is an amazing woman. She is hardworking, committed to her children, generous with her grandchildren, firm in her convictions, and energetic in her determination to make a positive difference in the lives of individuals who are physically or mentally challenged. Watching her get behind a cause and implement a plan is like watching a one-person army move a whole platoon into formation for the desired aim. She gets things done!

At the age of seventeen she found herself pregnant and unmarried. On the day of that baby's birth, her own mother walked into the room, looked at the infant in her daughter's arms and said, "For the last nine months I prayed that this child would be born dead."

When I heard this story, I felt weak in the knees and faint in my heart. You see, the baby my mother-in-law was holding in her arms that day is my husband today. If Grandma had gotten her wish then, I would have missed out on marrying an incredible man. I'm able to tell the story now since Grandma has passed on. She was filled with the fear of facing her friends and family with the news of a child conceived out of wedlock. Mom married the father of her child and as time passed, Grandma did grow to love the grandchild she had rejected earlier.

Thinking about my mother-in-law's situation, I wondered how she was ever able to face her past and get on with her future in such a successful way. In spite of the initial disapproval and condemnation from her own mother, she became confident, energized, focused, and determined to look on the positive side of a negative life situation.

I wondered about the fears she had faced in the past. What gave her the courage to get beyond the shame, rage, bitterness, and pain? How does *anyone* find "life" beyond the damaging events and hurtful memories of the past?

Triggering event: There must have been a growing fear when Mom began to suspect she was an unwed, pregnant teenager. I'm sure the fear was deepened on the day the suspicion became a known fact.

Reactive emotion: Grandpa was a tall, gruff, authoritarian, controlling man. Mom must have been filled with terror at the thought of telling her parents about the pregnancy. What would the family think? Her fears went far beyond the initial panic. If she married the father of the baby, it would calm her parents down a bit. But would it be the *right* decision for her and for the child in her womb? How could she support herself and this baby?

Powerlessness: One of the most debilitating aspects of fear is its ability to sap our strength, drain our energy, confuse our ability to make wise choices, and rob us of confidence. To be powerless is to experience a void at several levels. Suddenly, we have no control over our own situation, no inner strength for hard times, no physical stamina to carry on with routine activities, and no hope that our dark cloud will lift. Instead of focusing on God and a spiritual resolution to our fear, we seem incapable of focusing on anything but our own loss of control.

Rage: When we get tired of being victimized by our own bad choices or by the pain inflicted upon us by people we trusted, anger replaces the sense of powerlessness. Sometimes the anger seethes within us, and others don't see it. But at other times, the fury of our rage surprises us with its outward intensity. One woman expressed it this way: "I was so shocked to hear my mother's angry voice coming out of *my* mouth!"

When it comes to the fear of facing our past, our anger seems to be highly selective in *who* it targets. At times, we are extremely angry with *ourselves*—reasoning that if we had been smarter or stronger, we could have stopped the person or event triggering our fear. At other times, we get angry at *the people who caused our pain.* If they had cared more about us and less about themselves, we would not have been in bondage to all of this fear. Finally, we direct our anger at *God.* Where was He when questionable situations emerged and when these people exhibited wrongful power over us? Where was He when we were tempted to make bad choices? Why didn't the sovereign God of the universe do something?

When we get angry because fear has stripped us of our power, we have a deep desire to become self-reliant, since relying on other people or on God hasn't seemed to help at all.

Internal negotiating: In our anger and sense of betrayal, we begin our "fix-it" program with internal negotiations. Feeling let down by other people and by God sends us into an internal battle. We are sick and tired of being controlled by fear, and *something* has to change or we will break down emotionally.

This a crucial point—because each of us has to face our own past. Will we rigidly choose a destructive resolution for our fear, or will we be willing to explore the depth of painful feelings our fear has produced and discover the path to wholeness?

Mom's choice: I have never wanted to pry into the details of what transpired between my mother-in-law and Grandma during the days following the birth of the baby Grandma disapproved of, but I assume that Mom chose a constructive resolution for dealing with her early fears. How do I know? Because I've observed her making faith-filled decisions on a regular basis for many years—and that takes practice!

THE DESTRUCTIVE CHOICES OF UNRESOLVED FEAR

Often, as we think about our fears, we rationalize about *why* certain things happened. Sometimes we come up with questions that have no answers:

- Why didn't I set an earlier curfew for my daughter?
- Why did I always give in to peer pressure?
- Why did I allow myself to get involved with a married man?

- Why did I take the first drink?
- Couldn't I have stopped the incest earlier?
- Why did I steal from my employer?
- Why did I listen to the abortion counselor instead of following my own convictions?
- Why did I destroy her reputation?
- Why did I sacrifice my virginity in order to be accepted?
- Why did I become a slave to my church instead of looking to God for my self-worth?
- Why did I stay in a job I hated for twenty years?

When we get no answers to those questions, we often seek a destructive course of action for dealing with the fears that resurface. We can sometimes convince ourselves to *deny* there was ever a fear in the first place. More often, we feel *defeated* by the fears from the past that haunt us today. In time, we successfully convince ourselves that the future will only be another version of a terrible past.

Sometimes we blame all the negatives in our lives on the events, people, and situations that caused us to fear in the first place. At this point *bitterness* takes over. Larry Crabb says, "Bitterness develops when people don't respond to our demands."[1] Sometimes our bitterness drives us to seek revenge on the institutions or individuals who caused our pain. At other times, we have a negative attitude toward life itself: "I've been dealt a bad hand—and I will *never* be able to overcome the pain in my past."

The end result for many of us is escape into obsessive/addictive patterns. We run from the past by jumping into too much work, exercise, or perfectionism. Each of these addictions wins us the applause of the crowd and momentarily our inner void is forgotten. But when the negative escapes turn us toward alcohol, codependency, and eating disorders, we discover we're stuck in a bottomless pit.

↗ LOOKING BACK AT YESTERDAY

Sometimes I wonder if I can ever get beyond the damage of the past. Is there any way to let go of the shame, rage, bitterness, pain, and anger? Is there any way to let the past become part of my life in a positive way—to use yesterday's mistakes and wrong choices to become part of the hope I have to offer others?

One of my major fears from the past deals with losing my second child in the early stages of pregnancy. The complete story of the miscarriage is told in my book *Secret Longings of the Heart*. After I experienced the loss of this much-wanted child, fear enveloped me. I had been warned to slow down, rest more often, reduce my schedule, and take care of my body. But in my drive to carry on with ministry responsibilities and do "important work for God," it did not seem prudent to slow my pace. Slowing down felt like a sign of weakness. I wanted to prove to myself and everybody else that I was *not* going to use pregnancy as an excuse for taking it easy.

And I lost the baby in the middle of a hectic schedule. Instead of seeking help when the cramps began, I continued to drive to my speaking engagement. Instead of calling for assistance, I walked to the ladies' room alone—and in the middle of a run-down community center restroom, I sat in a stall surrounded by graffiti and filth, while my baby, just in the embryo stages of life, spontaneously left my womb.

I have lived with the guilt of wondering if I could have saved that little life if I had followed the doctor's instructions more carefully. Often, our lives are made up of *afterthoughts*.

- If only I could live that one day over . . .
- If only I hadn't married the first man who showed an interest in me . . .
- If only I had taken the other route home . . .

- If only I could take back those words of criticism . . .
- If only I could erase that one night from existence . . .
- If only I had left that miserable job earlier . . .
- If only I had resisted the flirtations of that man . . .
- If only I had spent more time with my children . . .
- If only I had understood that I was the victim . . .
- If only I hadn't waited so long to have children . . .

When we allow ourselves to look back at the past and meditate on all of those "if onlys," we wind up being victimized by guilt and shame for much of our adult lives. The enemy boldly articulates his message of fear, despair, and hopelessness. He wants to convince us there is no God of love and that we are damaged beyond repair. This is the worst fear of all! It's not just the past events that are so scary, but it's the fact that the memories of past events and mistakes we've made bring up our feelings of worthlessness.

13 UNDERSTANDING GUILT AND SHAME

If competitions were held for "Guilt Queen of the Year," many of us would be in the running. Sometimes it makes us feel better to take the full responsibility for *why* our lives are so miserable. Most of us have never wanted to be negative women who grovel in our mistakes, but when life isn't turning out right we eagerly take the blame.

Someone once told me the definition of *mounting apprehension*. It's the feeling experienced by a pet who is owned by a taxidermist! I think guilt is a lot like that. God certainly isn't a taxidermist who is going to take our lives when we are no longer useful to Him, but He does have power over us. We know a "day of reckoning" is coming. We feel mounting apprehension about the mistakes of the past. What gets confusing is figuring out if we've brought the problem on ourselves. Our anxiety continues to grow until we've convinced ourselves we could have done *something* to stop whatever happened. In time, shame often replaces guilt.

In his book *Restoring Innocence,* Alfred Ells says,

> The single most hurtful legacy many families leave their children is shame. . . . Where guilt says, "I made a mistake," shame says, "I *am* the mistake." Shame is often an excruciating and punishing awareness of one's own insufficiency and inadequacy, and it is probably the most painful emotion one can experience.[2]

The shame felt so deeply by women who were sexually abused is a false shame, but they don't know it. It feels real. It follows them everywhere. And if they experienced any sexual pleasure during the process of being victimized, they often cling to shame. But it's illegitimate shame—a trick of our enemy to place them in confusion and bewilderment.

Though we may not be dealing with the heavy burden of sexual abuse, we *are* dealing with the mistakes of our former days. We know our bad choices caused someone else pain. We know we made errors in judgment that hurt our Christian testimony. We know there is no way to take back words that have already been spoken or to undo a wrongful deed. We know there is no way to bring life back to an aborted child. There's no way to relive a day of life that is already history.

As we get the courage to face the past in order to get on with the future, we need to understand the difference between *illegitimate shame* and *legitimate shame.* Simply stated, false shame accepts the blame for inappropriate things. It causes thinking like this: "If I could have controlled someone's drinking, he wouldn't have had the accident," or "If I had been more obedient, this evil thing would not have happened."

Conversely, legitimate shame is facing our failure to trust God with the healing of our souls. That level of humility is the basis of our return to the Father.[3] We experience deep sorrow over the evil that has been done to us during victimization, which brings us to brokenness before God. For example, legitimate shame does not lead to confession for our role in childhood abuse. The child was the victim. Legitimate shame leads to humility before God as we acknowledge our sinful self-reliance—our efforts to run from the pain or to protect ourselves from the God who seems to have let us down.

Whether our pain is caused by victimization or by our own mistakes and wrong choices, we have a natural tendency to rely on ourselves to get out of a distressing situation. Our immediate reaction is to escape our pain and look for an antidote—which usually leads us down the destructive path of denial, defeat, bitterness, or compulsive behavior. The best course of action, even though we often don't see it at first glance, is to allow our pain to lead us back to God.

13 THE BENEFITS OF PAIN

I'm not very good at allowing myself to *experience* the depth of past pain. I would much rather read a book on how to manage my problem or read a success story about someone else who overcame obstacles. But looking into the face of my own shame, guilt, unforgiveness, or personal sorrow is too frightening!

C. S. Lewis once said, "Pain insists on being attended to. God whispers to us in our pleasures, speaks to us in our conscience, but shouts in our pains. It is His megaphone to rouse a deaf world."[4] Exploring our feelings is always frightening. Old wounds fester. Relationships that are now tolerable are once again threatened. Plastic smiles fade. Honesty replaces the game of "let's pretend." Long-hidden fears resurface. Our past "shadow monsters" make images on the wall of our minds and bring flickers of dreaded emotion.

When we choose a constructive resolution for our fears, *sorrow* is the first major step. It's important to grieve over the injustices of the past, the mistakes we've made, and the consequences we've brought on ourselves. The first step to a faith-filled decision is to acknowledge the deep pain we have experienced.

David Biebel describes the greatest benefit of pain: "The old center has collapsed, and I am helpless."[5] In other words, instead of following our former, rigid path of handling our emotions and taking care of our problems, we begin to yield. We acknowledge that our system for dealing with fear failed and we cannot "fix" things ourselves.

Many of us are in bondage to the memories of our mistakes or to the reminders of the violations by others. When we allow ourselves to grieve over injustices and bad memories, our sorrow brings us to the place of *brokenness* that has just been described. Our old center (everything we could do to fix our problems) has collapsed—and we are helpless.

One day while reading the Sermon on the Mount I came to the verse where Jesus says, "Blessed are the poor in spirit, for theirs is the kingdom of heaven" (Matthew 5:3, NIV). I had always assumed that the phrase "poor in spirit" had something to do with being needy, but after further study, I saw the verse in a whole new light.

Jesus was saying, "You are right on target if you have quit relying on your own dynamic personality, your personal wealth, or your grand accomplishments to get you into heaven. You are truly blessed if you have come to the end of your resources—and you can admit you are needy." In other words, a spirit of humility is the first step toward spiritual wholeness—and that level of humility often comes after we grieve over injustices and wrong choices and when we experience true brokenness before God.

Brokenness turns to surrender when we say, "Lord, I can no longer pick myself up by my own bootstraps. I *need* You and I surrender myself to You—my pain, my bad memories, my mistakes, my disappointments, and my expectations. I will choose to stop living with the fearful shadow monsters of the past. I willfully hang my weakness on Your almighty strength."

⌀ A FAITH-FILLED DECISION TO FORGIVE

Much of our ability to face the past in order to get on with the future is wrapped up in the power of forgiveness. Surrender to God brings us to the point of being able to make the faith-filled decision to forgive.

When we choose unforgiveness for the injustices of the past, we hurt ourselves most of all. Booker T. Washington once said, "I will not permit any man to narrow and degrade my soul by making me hate him."[6] I think Washington knew that the opposite of forgiveness was to put himself in bondage to those who had wronged him—to be powerless and fearful of injustice. To forgive is to be set free!

Author Judith Sills wrote,

> Forgive, and you free all the energy you are currently using in reviewing old injuries, fantasizing revenge, craving justice.
> Forgive, and the piece of you that was tied up with rage is free to be much, much more. . . .
>
> Forgiveness is not approval. . . . Forgiveness says, "What you did hurt me deeply and you were wrong to do it. I have hated you for what you did long enough. Now I want to let go of my hatred. I forgive you."[7]

The concept of forgiveness is so powerful that we can understand it only by experiencing it. Most of us have no idea how much control we give to people who have hurt us or wronged us by allowing them to rob us of weeks, months, even years of happy, productive lives. When our days are consumed with thoughts of revenge, or a recounting of the abuses of the past, or a rehearsed itemization of why we hate ourselves for the wrong choices we have made, we are chaining ourselves in a prison of our own making.

For a lesson in forgiveness, look at Jesus. Nail-pierced hands. A crown of thorns. No complaint coming from His lips. No blaming accusations hurled at His abusers. That day Innocence hung on a cross. Injustice prevailed. Pushing up on nails in His feet to get the breath to speak, He uttered the most empowering words in Scripture: "Father, forgive them, for they know not what they do."

I think of my mother-in-law. Grandma's words to her after the birth of her infant son reverberate in my mind: "For the last nine months I prayed that this child would be born dead."

What gave Mom the grace to make a faith-filled decision to choose a constructive resolution for the fears that plagued her? I believe she grieved over the injustice of the situation—and probably over her own questionable choices. But I believe that sorrow led to brokenness, which brought humility before God that led to *surrender* of her will. This surrender gave Mom the power to make the *faith-filled decision* to forgive her mother and forgiveness freed her from the bondage of the past.

⅓ TAMING OUR "SHADOW MONSTERS"

Facing the truth involves seeing our fears as they really are.

- Have we exaggerated our fears of the past?
- Have we run from past fears, hoping they will disappear?
- Do we carry any false guilt or illegitimate shame?
- Have we grieved over the injustice in our lives and experienced the sorrow of painful memories?

- Have we chosen the empowering freedom of forgiveness?
- Have we looked back at Calvary lately? Hear Jesus once again: "Father, forgive them, for they know not what they do."

Occasionally, I try to "take back" fearful memories. As my shadow monsters resurface on my movies of the past, I hear His reassuring voice in the middle of the darkness. "Let go, Carol. I'll see you in the morning."

"HOW CAN I HAVE THESE DOUBTS ABOUT GOD AND CALL MYSELF A CHRISTIAN?"

Fear 8: Losing My Faith

> *For every confirmed skeptic I encounter, I meet at least a dozen sincere believers who struggle with doubt. At times their apprehension is casual, but at other times it is grave. These people want to believe God, but for whatever reason, wrestle with thoughts and feelings to the contrary. And, unfortunately, when doubt enters the believer's experience it threatens to paralyze him.*
>
> JOSH MCDOWELL
> Quoted by Jackie Hudson in the foreword of
> *Doubt, A Road to Growth*

Jackie Hudson had spent years of her life in full-time Christian service with a well-known international ministry. She was vitally involved in helping with the preparations for EXPLO, a conference that was designed to train over 80,000 Christians in principles of evangelism and discipleship.

When the first day of the event finally arrived, she watched the crowd spilling onto the playing field of the Cotton Bowl in Dallas. Without warning, a frightening and foreign thought flashed through her mind: "How do all these people really know there is a God?" Jackie describes an avalanche of thoughts:

> I was stunned. Did I think that? After all, I'm one of the 250 staff members working on this evangelism training conference. We've planned and prayed and worked for months for this. I'm in full-time Christian work! How can I think a thought like that?[1]

During the next few weeks Jackie tried to push the haunting thoughts out of her mind. But to no avail. She was drowning in a sea of doubt.

> Questions engulfed my mind. How do I know God exists? Is the Bible really His inspired Word? What about the 2.5 billion people who have never heard about Christ? Are they going to hell? That seems so unfair![2]

Jackie had great difficulty eating and sleeping. Anxiety and panic became her constant companions. Skepticism and uncertainty replaced faith and assurance. In desperation Jackie confessed her doubt to God, memorized lengthy passages of Scripture, and asked for help from Christian friends. But the doubts stubbornly persisted. "Maybe I'm not really a Christian, I thought. Maybe I can't believe because I'm not one of the 'chosen ones.'"[3]

Jackie had heard someone say that if you're not *sure* you're a Christian, you should pray one final time and write the date in your Bible. That way, when the doubts come, you can look the date up and be reminded of the time when the commitment was made. As she scanned the front of her

Bible, Jackie found *five* different dates when she had prayed "the prayer"—just to be certain! But the doubts returned.

✍ WHY DO WE KEEP OUR DOUBTS A SECRET?

Christians who are struggling with doubts about their faith almost never talk about it. They are too ashamed. And if they are Christian leaders—especially if they receive financial support from other believers—to admit their intense fear is to risk being fired from a ministry position, followed by malicious gossip and bankruptcy. Who would want to give money to support a missionary or worker who had doubts about Christian theology?

So with no one to turn to, the doubts increase, and the fear is magnified. For most of us, it becomes easier to live a lie and to fake confidence than to say, "I'm struggling. In fact, I'm having major questions about things I've believed for years. My doubts are plaguing me, and I don't know what to do."

Are we are afraid that if we admit doubts about God—or about heaven or hell or the supernatural—we will become infidels and traitors? If we have no one to talk to, we stay locked up, hurting, uncertain, fearful, and in some cases, paralyzed. This mental and spiritual imprisonment is based on the fear of facing the naked truth of all that is raging in our minds and hearts.

✍ WHAT KINDS OF DOUBTS DO WE HAVE?

I've heard women ask riveting questions related to the fear of losing their faith. The first entry on this list came from one of my former junior high students who as a grown woman came to visit me, ten years after she sat in my classroom.

- "Carol, you led me to Jesus when I was in the eighth grade. All these years I've kept a secret from you. My mother was extremely abusive, and my father was an alcoholic who was uninvolved in my life. In my teen years, mostly in order to escape from my unhappy home, I became close to another woman and developed a lesbian relationship with her. I became hopelessly involved in homosexuality, and it has a grip on my life. I know the Bible teaches against this lifestyle, and I've tried to quit a hundred times — but I always go back. I have *begged* God to take this curse from me, but He doesn't. Is the God I trusted in the eighth grade still alive?"

- "I used to believe in a loving God, but since I saw those planes crash into the World Trade Center, I have trouble trusting in a God who allows innocent people to die."

- "I made a childhood decision to accept Christ, but now I wonder if I'm really a Christian."

- "I have prayed for my children since they were in my womb. They were raised in a loving home and given every opportunity for spiritual growth and encouragement. In spite of all the positive, Christian input, my son has dropped out of school and is addicted to cocaine. My teenage daughter is an unwed mother. Is there really a God who hears and answers prayers?"

- "I went to a university of higher learning for a specific purpose — to enjoy the parties, the wide variety of gorgeous men, and to experience the freedom from parental control. My weekends were filled with alcohol, drugs, and promiscuity. Then I met Jesus through a campus ministry — and He totally changed my desires and my lifestyle. Two years later I was engaged to a vibrant Christian man when I discovered I not only had two different kinds of venereal diseases — I was also infected with the HIV virus. *Why* would God allow this to happen?"

- "My earliest memory dates back to when I was five years old. I was being violently raped by a male relative. By the time I was old enough to leave home, I had been sexually abused by my grandfather, father, brothers, and a few male cousins. I can name twelve men who victimized me. Today I find it impossible to receive love properly from my husband. The thought of physical intimacy makes me sick. If God exists, why would He let a child be damaged so badly?"

- "I was raised in a Christian home, but after doing some of my university studies overseas and since being exposed to several large and diverse world religions, I'm having real doubts that there is only *one* way to get to heaven. The God I believe in would not let all of those sincere, religious people go to hell—just because they don't believe in Jesus Christ."

- "My husband has been unemployed for two years, and I was just pink-slipped. We have used our entire savings account, and if this goes six more months every dime saved for our retirement will be spent on household necessities. We have always tithed our income, giving God the 'first fruits,' but now I'm beginning to doubt Him. We've given to Him all these years, but our whole world is falling apart—and it appears He is unconcerned."

⅓ DISAPPOINTMENT WITH GOD

Perhaps the most haunting thought a Christian woman can ever have is this: *What if the beliefs I have always held about God, the faith I have affirmed to others, and the beliefs I have taught my children are inaccurate? If the Bible has errors, if God is not real, if my convictions are faulty, or if there is no heaven or hell—I am left with absolutely nothing to give lasting purpose to my life.* The thought of having a meaningless life, void of supernatural strength, biblical counsel, and hope for an eternal life is so devastating that we often prefer to live with our unspoken doubts, pushing them down into our subconscious, rather than risk voicing them and wrestling with them.

What expectations did you have when you "signed on" to become a Christ-follower? I'm sure many of us thought we could anticipate health, wealth, joy, love, peace, adventure, contentment, and happiness. We knew Christianity was supposed to offer a new, satisfying, more fulfilling life.

Perhaps the biggest expectation was having a direct line to God. We knew He would be available on the tough days and during the major decisions. We expected a personal protector to shield us from doubt, discouragement, and despair. But our expectations sometimes become bitter disappointments.

Ken Abraham, in a soul-searching book called *The Disillusioned Christian*, says,

> Nobody ever warned you that there would be times when God seemed a million miles away. Or you might pray for somebody to be healed and they would die. Where were those financial blessings when you needed them, like when it came time to pay the rent? And what about all those great Christian superstars who have let you down?[4]

As we look back at the fears voiced earlier, we see a whole list of disappointed disciples, women who doubt God's goodness, power, or wisdom because of the suffering they observe in the world or experience daily. Others are disappointed because God hasn't made them the faith- and joy-filled women they expected. Still others are disappointed that so many people of other faiths seem to be as decent and reasonable as the Christians they know.

♫ THE GIFT OF DOUBT

Philip Yancey once said, "Fear, not doubt, is faith's opposite." In other words, if we are willing to look into the face of doubt, seeking truth (not fearing it), we will find a renewed faith. When we shrink back, unwilling to face legitimate doubt about the truth of God's Word, the justice of God's plan, and the disappointments in our lives—we live in a fearful cage of growing disillusionment.

Many of us have believed the only answer to doubt is to confess it as sin and to decide, once and for all, never to doubt again. But on a closer look, it's easy to see a hidden destructive pattern in this decision.

Sometimes when we follow this course, it looks like this: Our *triggering event* could be the loss of an unborn child, a severe financial reversal, or huge doubts about the goodness of God. We respond with an overwhelming *reactive emotion:* terror that we'll lose our faith in the God we have always trusted. Our sense of *powerlessness* is foreign. We have always counted on God for guidance and comfort. But we certainly sense no supernatural help in our situation. He seems to be out of the picture. It appears He doesn't care. As we focus on our desperate condition, we turn to *rage*. How could the God we looked to for protection, love, and guidance all these years let us down? If He is real, why doesn't He make Himself more obvious? Our focus has now moved from God to ourselves, and our self-reliance leads to *internal negotiating*.

♫ THE RIGID RESOLUTION

If that internal battle leads to a destructive course of action, it follows a rigid, uncompromising path. For the woman who makes this negative choice, there are four different potential end results.

1. *Denial*—When we follow the path of confessing our doubt as sin, telling ourselves we will never talk about our doubt again, determining

never to question the goodness of God, we live in denial. It's almost like saying, "God, if I really investigated my doubts, I might find out something that would destroy my faith completely, and I just can't risk that!"

2. *Defeat*—Defeat leads us to abandon faith. It closes the door to hope and makes our world smaller and smaller. We feel let down by God, Christian friends, and biblical principles. We allow our disappointment with God to lead to a final decision of, "Lord, I'm giving up on You, the Bible, the church, and Christian friends. I quit!"

3. *Bitterness*—A sense of betrayal leads to bitterness. When we have given our lives to God and have worked for Him and taught His principles as truth—and He allows injustice, misery, poor health, infertility, and deep disappointment to enter our lives—we sometimes choose bitterness.

When bitterness takes root, we begin to believe a lie: God has dealt me a bad hand. He picked me out of all the other Christians and betrayed me by allowing deep hurts and injustices to rob me of my faith.

4. *Escape*—In an attempt to ease the pain caused by a void that now exists where faith used to be, we sometimes cling to a diversion that provides momentary relief from our fear of being rejected by God and left without hope. Depending on our personality and background, we choose from a wide range of obsessive/compulsive behaviors. From perfectionism to alcohol to workaholism to prescription drugs to *anything* that can cover up the festering wound of a broken spirit and a disillusioned heart. Our unspoken response is, "God has deserted me, and I will fill up the vacuum in my soul. I can fix this need myself. I don't need Him anymore!"

13 THE DAY THE ACCELERATOR STUCK

I had been married about six months. My husband, Gene, and I had moved to Grand Rapids, Michigan. Gene was taking some graduate classes, and I was working as an executive secretary for the Steelcase Corporation.

One morning on my way to work in rush-hour traffic, my accelerator stuck as I was approaching a red light. No matter how hard I pressed my foot to the brake, my car picked up speed. As I swerved into an open lane, I had difficulty guiding my fast-moving vehicle to make the turn, and I hit the car waiting to make a left-hand turn—and that car hit the car behind it.

As my car continued on I glanced at the gas gauge. It was half full. Thinking quickly, I knew I could not run the car out of gas before causing a horrible accident in the next intersection. After trying the emergency brake to no avail, in a desperate attempt to stop the car, I steered the automobile toward a telephone pole before evacuating. The car hit the curb, missing the pole, and went right into the next intersection and hit another car, which hit the car behind it. (That's a five car collision so far!) It did a circle in the intersection and then pulled out a fire hydrant, did another circle in the intersection and destroyed a park bench, and did one more circle before crashing into the plate-glass window of the prestigious IBM building.

Police sirens descended and after listening to my explanation of what happened, an officer said, "Why didn't you turn the ignition off?" I never thought of it. The day after this horrible experience we discovered we had no insurance. When we left the Christian organization my husband and I worked for previously, they "gifted us" with six additional months of insurance, but due to a clerical mistake, we were uninsured for this disastrous accident.

Two women sustained minor injuries, and we were grateful there was no loss of life—but the property damage was extensive! We were dirt poor, still paying off education loans, and the day after we made the second large payment to our attorney (with borrowed money), the newspaper ran an article on *our* attorney. It read, in part, "This man has been disbarred from practicing law in the State of Michigan because of indecent exposure in his office."

We were financially ruined, emotionally exhausted, and spiritually devastated! We were in a brand-new marriage and suddenly all of the hopes, aspirations, plans, and dreams we had for the future were crushed by the fear of what the next phone call would tell us.

✍ THE QUESTIONS WE ARE AFRAID TO ASK

Looking back, it's easy for me to see the *triggering event* that caused my initial fear. In a fast-moving car that was out of control I feared for my life. My *reactive emotions* brought the fear of financial ruin, the fear of abandonment by God, and the hidden fear of losing my confidence in the God I had always trusted to meet my needs. My sense of *powerlessness* became overwhelming when we discovered our insurance had been mistakenly transferred to another vehicle by the Christian organization we had served so faithfully.

When my focus gets off God and on my problems—watch out! I turned to *rage*. As a "slow boiler," I didn't express my anger on the surface immediately, but I was mad! How could the organization we had served with such loyalty let something like this happen? But the anger intensified when I thought about my all-knowing God who should have been overseeing this situation more carefully!

I remained in the "rage stage" for a long time. I was mad at the Christians who made the mistake on my insurance. I was mad at the "Statute of Limitations" in Michigan that allowed cases concerning this accident to be brought to court for up to seven years! I was mad at God. This disappointment led to *internal negotiating:*

- Why would a God of love allow this to happen? Gene and I had dedicated our lives to Him, but we faced more red lights than green lights.

- Why did God allow a young Christian couple in the middle of their first year of marriage to have such an avalanche of financial problems—through no fault of their own?
- Why didn't the God of the universe "fix" the stuck accelerator? Where was He when the car was out of control and I was yelling for help?
- If God couldn't be trusted to protect the people most eager to serve Him, why should we rely on Him in the future?

13 RESOLVING TO BELIEVE

For the first time in my Christian life, I began to doubt the goodness of God. With that came an erosion of what had been strong faith. I felt betrayed by the God I had served with pure motives and energetic service. I never got to the fear of losing all faith in God, but I faced unanswerable questions that left me uncomfortable and immobile as a Christian. It's at this point many women choose the destructive resolution. The rigid choice brings on denial, defeat, bitterness, or escape.

But I had another alternative. I remember talking at length with my husband and voicing my doubts about God out loud for the first time. It was freeing to admit that I felt God had been unfair to us and that He didn't seem to be answering prayer or intervening in our situation at all.

After a long time, I knelt beside a kitchen chair with my husband at my side, and my internal negotiating finally moved to genuine *sorrow.* I told God how disappointed I was. I voiced my doubts about His love. I spoke of my anger for what appeared to be unjust treatment. I told Him how unfair it felt to be in financial limbo for seven years—knowing *everything* we owned could be taken away from us with one lawsuit. I allowed myself to grieve over the financial devastation of the accident and for the lawyer who had taken our money unethically. My sorrow soon turned to *brokenness*. We were in a mess, and it was too big for me to solve. In spite of my pain and doubt, I knew I needed God's help through all of this. I humbled myself before Him, giving up the deep desire I had to control the situation myself.

This led to a *surrender* I had never known before. I stopped telling God how to change my situation. My heart began to believe the words as I prayed, "Lord, I submit myself to Your authority. I choose to trust You—even if in this lifetime I am never allowed to understand why You have allowed this terrible accident to happen. I believe You still love me." I was surprised by my own words.

This constructive resolution to fear brings us to an ability to make *faith-filled decisions*. Paula Rinehart describes the faith that emerges out of broken dreams:

> "How is faith that comes on the far side of disappointment better than (the) faith that preceded it?" . . . There is room for mystery—for *not* knowing all the answers. The passage of faith that follows disillusionment begins when there is no experiential reason to believe. It is born in the fearlessness that comes when you've already lost a good portion of what you were so afraid of losing in the first place.[5]

This process defies being understood until it is experienced. It's part of the mystery—and part of the inexplicable freedom from the fear of losing my confidence in God. In the middle of the journey, I stumble over the answer to one of my lifelong questions: *Where is God when I'm in pain?*

> Somehow, you know God is there in the midst of this passage—in ways you didn't expect. He makes His presence known by the

pain of His seeming absence. He doesn't necessarily change the circumstances; He gives you the courage to face and move through them.[6]

In time, I was able to see some of the many beneficial effects of the accident. I made some faith-filled, though at times humbling, decisions:

- I gave up my "I'll-do-it-myself" attitude and allowed some of God's people to help meet severe financial needs.
- I better identified with the many people I had ministered to who had experienced doubts about God and their faith.
- I let myself feel the pangs of living in a fallen world, filled to the brim with disappointments and unfulfilled expectations.
- I learned to be thankful for the grace of God in the middle of the disaster. Each time a lawsuit reached the courthouse, I was declared innocent of any wrongdoing. The report read: "The accelerator was stuck, and the driver did everything in her power to stop the vehicle." So in spite of years of attorneys' fees, we were spared huge financial liability for multiple lawsuits.
- I learned the importance of talking out loud about my doubts, fears, and discouragements. One of the greatest benefits of the accident has been the lesson learned on my knees at the kitchen chair: Doubts about God need not lead to denial, defeat, bitterness, or escape. Instead they can lead to a "truth-search." Asking questions related to our doubts will lead to a strengthened faith as we discover truth in the process.

I long to reach a plateau in my spiritual experience that ensures I will never doubt again—a faith that promises I will never question God's truth or love or goodness. But in this world, that would be idyllic.

Gary Parker mirrors my thoughts:

When our faith in God transcends our doubts about God, we will
not find, in the same moment, the key that unlocks the door to
all of life's mysteries. . . . And we will not find solutions to all of
life's problems or acquire protection against all of life's tragedies.
We will, however, find a framework for life that brings purpose to
our days, meaning to our hearts, and solace to our hurts. We will
find a spiritual Father in whom we can place our trust.[7]

This level of trust involves risk and uncertainty that can be transcended
by a faith that gives us an eternal perspective.

13 PETER LEARNED THE SECRET

Peter is often described as the "open mouth, insert foot" disciple. He spoke
before he thought. He sometimes acted without thinking through the consequences. He was quick to speak, slow to listen. But, at times, this spon-
taneous personality had to be refreshing to Jesus. He never had to guess
what Peter was thinking.

The account in John 6 says that people were following Jesus. Anywhere
this man went, exciting action followed! Think of it. He fed the five thousand with one little boy's lunch. Some of these "new disciples" were following because of the incredible miracles. Others joined the group for free
food. Jesus rebukes them and says, "I tell you the truth, you are looking for
me, not because you saw miraculous signs but because you ate the loaves
and had your fill" (John 6:26, NIV).

Then Jesus began teaching in word pictures. He talked about the Bread
of Life. And He said *He* is *the living bread,* and if anyone eats of this bread,

that person will live forever. That was too much for some of the "fringe followers." After Jesus explained the meaning of this statement, many of these
disciples grumbled and some said, "This is a hard teaching. Who can accept
it?" (John 6:60, NIV).

It reminds me of an elementary teacher who assigned book reports on
an animal story. She got back one report that was only one line long. It said,
"This book tells more about penguins than I want to know!"

I think some of those disciples were a lot like that student. They *loved*
hanging around Jesus while there was drama and excitement—but when
tough teaching came, they were through! Imagine how they might have
voiced their thoughts: "This man gives me more confusing information
than I'm interested in hearing. I wish He'd stick to miracles and quit talking in riddles."

The contrasts in that crowd tell the whole story. They were seeking a
circus. Jesus was offering truth. They demanded outward drama. Jesus
sought inward change. They looked for a hero. Jesus came to be a servant.
When they did not get what they wanted, many of those brand-new disciples packed up their marbles and went home.

At that moment Jesus turned to the Twelve and said, "Do you also want
to leave?" And Peter, in typical, fast-responding and enthusiastic form, said,
"Master, to whom would we go? You have the words of real life, eternal life.
We've already committed ourselves, confident that you are the Holy One of
God" (John 6:67-69).

Peter went on to deny Jesus three times—but over time his early conviction took root. Read the story in the epistles Peter wrote later on. He
wrote to Christians who were hurting. They were scattered in the five
provinces of the Roman Empire. The heat had been turned up on these
believers. In the 105 verses of 1 Peter, the word *suffering* appears sixteen
times. They knew what persecution felt like.

If we look closely, Peter gives us the secret of an eternal perspective. He reminds us of two important faith-builders:

1. Our hope rests in the power of Christ's resurrection.
2. Our hope is fixed on the promise of our reward.

No matter what life dishes out along the way, there is nowhere to go but to Christ! Peter's entire challenge to people in pain involved reminding them they were pilgrims—people who were just passing through this fallen world. Then he helped them focus on "goin' home."

Think of it. One day doubts and fears will all be in the past. We will be in a kingdom that cannot be shaken. No more unanswerable questions. No more unexplainable suffering. No more riveting doubts. No more paralyzing fear. We will see Him as He is. As we look at the nail prints, we will finally understand.

"WHAT IF I NEVER LIVE UP TO MY POTENTIAL?"

Fear 9: Getting Trapped

/3

In the middle of our lives, from about ages thirty-five to forty-five, our marriages and careers have generally settled into a routine. This is a time when many women question their life choices and ask, Is that all there is?

JEAN LUSH
Emotional Phases of a Woman's Life

As early as I can remember, I always wanted to make a difference in the lives of other people. I desired to be a woman of vision, passion, and commitment. As a teenager I had made a covenant with my best friend, Janet. We were both idealistic, empowered with youthful enthusiasm—but we were serious. We decided that if Jesus Christ was who He claimed to be, He was worth *everything* we had to give Him. We made a commitment to hold each other accountable for becoming Christian women who would change our corner of the world in a positive way for the sake of God's kingdom.

In my quest for meaning, I began collecting quotations that inspired me to pursue God's highest and best calling. Some of my favorites follow:

- Choose a goal for which you are willing to exchange a piece of your life.
- When I come to the end of my life, will it have mattered that I was here?
- What makes life worthwhile is having a big enough objective, something which catches our imagination and lays hold of our allegiance; and this the Christian has, in a way that no other man has.[1]

SEARCHING FOR THE "DOT"

With energy and idealism, I continued my quest to find the "dot" in the center of God's will for my life. After coming to Christ at my mother's knee at the age of five, I had often been instructed to seek God's "perfect plan" for my life. Being totally convinced there was an ideal blueprint was comforting. It meant if I could just find the right niche, difficult decisions and hard choices would no longer plague me. I would not have to be afraid of getting trapped in a losing situation or vocation. I wouldn't need to grieve over lost opportunity. I would be right on target for total happiness and contentment in my life—and I wanted that!

Finding God's "dot" was important to me. It would abolish the headaches brought on by heavy decisions. It would make me feel secure. It would eliminate the gripping fear of choosing a path of "second best." That was my worst fear—making choices because I felt indefinite about the "perfect" will of God and finding out years later that I should have followed a different path in order to please Him more fully.

I spent many hours meditating on Scripture, trying to make sure I didn't miss the right signals. I began to devour Bible passages that reinforced my belief in the "dot." Psalm 32:8 (KJV) was my favorite, and I immediately claimed it as my "life verse": "I will instruct thee and teach thee in the way which thou shalt go; I will guide thee with mine eye." Surely that verse meant that God was going to give me specific instructions. But where were they hidden?

Another passage I clung to was in Proverbs 3:5-6: "Trust GOD from the bottom of your heart; don't try to figure out everything on your own. Listen for GOD's voice in everything you do, everywhere you go; he's the one who will keep you on track." I delivered devotionals to my church youth group using these verses and challenging my friends to find the center of God's will. And I waited for God to tell me what His "straight path" for my life was.

13 THE FEAR OF A DEAD-END LIFE

As a visual thinker I am endowed with a powerful imagination! As a young woman about ready to leave home and make her mark on the world, I had nagging apprehensions about being sure I was making choices that would result in the use of my full potential. I was obsessed with the fear of getting trapped in a situation that would mean I had lost out on an "A" choice because "B+" looked good at the time.

I worried about what university to attend. A few years later I was anxious about whether or not I should get married. The day finally arrived—my wedding day. I had dated the man I was about to marry for four years. He appeared to be the ideal choice for a lifetime of fulfillment and joy. But as I sat in the home of my best friend before leaving for the church, panic struck.

With profound sincerity I articulated my fears: "Janet, it's not too late for me to back out of this marriage. Could I be ruining the rest of my life? It would be embarrassing to call everything off at this point. But I am so afraid of making the wrong decision. I wonder if God would use my gifts more fully if I remained single."

Some of the fears that came out of my "dot theology" went like this:

- If I attend the wrong college or university, I could meet people who will negatively influence my life.
- If I don't major in the right field, I could wind up in a job that is unfulfilling, beneath my potential, and out of God's will.
- If I don't marry God's ideal man for my life, I will totally ruin my life—and the lives of the man I was supposed to marry, the man I did marry, and the woman my husband was supposed to marry. (This thought got even more complicated as I pondered the birth of children and wondered if they too were "messed up for life" because of my wrong choice.)
- If I don't buy a home in God's choice of neighborhoods, I may lose out on meeting a neighbor God wanted me to win to the Lord. (At this point, I realized there was a flaw in my thinking—but I still didn't know what it was.)

One day I picked up a book that put me into shock. It asked questions I was afraid to think about. It attacked some beliefs about God's will that I held close to my heart. It was addressing fears that I had hidden deeply—fears I didn't want to admit. Even the title of the book sounded controversial: *Decision Making and the Will of God: A Biblical Alternative to the Traditional View.*

Garry Friesen, a Bible professor who had grappled with this major dilemma, voiced the same questions that had been flickering in my mind:

1. Does God have a perfect will for each Christian? Does it matter?
2. Does the Christian have the right to choose and still be in the will of God?

3. Can you be 100 percent sure of God's individual will for your life?[2]

Each of these questions revolved around my great fear—getting trapped outside of God's ideal plan for the potential He placed within me.

> If we ask, "How can I know the will of God?" we may be asking the wrong question. The Scriptures do not command us to find God's will for most of life's choices nor do we have any passage instructing us on how it can be determined . . . the Christian community has never agreed on how God provides us with such special revelation. Yet we persist in searching for God's will because decisions require thought and sap energy. We seek relief from the responsibility of decision making and we feel less threatened by being passive rather than active when making important choices.[3]

All of this made so much sense. I knew I was created in the image of God and that He had given me the ability to reason and think out the answers to perplexing problems. I held in my hands the completed Word of God. But I was still in quest of an easy way to find complete joy and fulfillment in life. I wanted "divine roadmarks"! Other people talked so confidently about receiving insight from God and about "signs" in the Bible that gave them specific direction. Was I wrong to expect the same thing?

FACING THE FEAR OF MAKING WRONG CHOICES

Many Christian women grapple with varying degrees of the identical problem. Here are some of the fears women have voiced regarding making wrong choices:

- If I can't get away from the ugliness of my past, I will be destined for failure.

- If I take *this* job now because of economic necessity, I may close the door on a better opportunity for career advancement in a position more suited to my background and education.

- If I don't work harder and outdo the competition in my office, I may not get a promotion.

- If I'm promoted, I may feel pressured to "succeed" at a level that will compromise balance in other important areas of my life.

- If I choose to marry, I may get a man as dysfunctional as my father, and I will never let that happen!

- If I don't marry *this* man, someone I'm more compatible with might not come along, and I'd be sorry I turned him down.

- If I *do* marry this man—even though we seem perfectly suited for one another—I may discover later I have shut myself out from reaching my highest potential in my work or ministry because of the "encumbrances" of marriage and family responsibilities.

- If I have a baby now, I may interrupt my career and never recapture the momentum and job success I've worked so hard to obtain.

- If I wait to have a child until I'm older and more established in my marriage and in my career, I may not be able to get pregnant.

- If I don't pursue infertility treatment, I will never know complete fulfillment as a mother and eventually, as a grandmother.

As I have listened to the heartfelt fears of so many women who struggle with the whole concept of "lost opportunity," one thought becomes predominant: All of us have an earnest desire to make choices that will result in personal fulfillment and spiritual satisfaction.

✍ LOOKING BACKWARD

How many times a week do we start a sentence with, "If only"?

- If only I could live this week over again . . .
- If only I had known what I know now . . .
- If only my dad (or mom) had not been an alcoholic . . .
- If only I had become a Christian earlier . . .
- If only I could have gotten a better education . . .
- If only I were as gifted as my sister (or brother) . . .
- If only I were married . . .
- If only I had married a different man . . .
- If only I had remained single . . .
- If only I could make that choice over again . . .

And often we believe in our hearts that it's much too late to change anything now.

> Does this sound familiar? Of course it does. Who among us can claim to have never made a mistake or missed a goal, never regretted a choice we made—or suffered because of someone else's action? Did you marry the wrong person? Take the wrong job? Fail to tell your mom how much you loved her before she died? Recognized opportunity only after you'd let it slide by? Did you goof not once but often? Do you get the feeling that it's become your way of life?[4]

Most of us have struggled with the fear of making wrong choices at some point in our lives. On certain days all of us feel trapped. And when we are changing dirty diapers, doing laundry, working in a job beneath our potential, or pouring so much of ourselves into work that we miss the rest of our lives, it's easy to envision ourselves as one of the few women in the world who is experiencing lost opportunity because of the options we've selected.

JANET'S MISSION

Janet changed my life. My best friend lived in a modest house on the other side of the railroad tracks. Her father was an alcoholic who was absent from her life—except for the handful of times he showed up on the doorstep looking for a handout. He offered Janet, her mother, and two sisters no financial or emotional support. They were on their own! Janet's mom worked in a local factory to put food on the table.

Both of Janet's sisters dropped out of high school and married at a young age. But not Janet. Wherever she went there was laughter—combined with deep discussions about life and God and the future. When I was with Janet, I felt full of hope.

Janet became the first person in her family to graduate from high school. She was the first to get a university degree and the only one to get a master's degree. Janet majored in elementary education because she wanted to give hope to kids who came from single-parent backgrounds like hers. She would look a struggling child in the eyes and say, "I didn't have a dad either. It sure is hard. But you can make it. I know you can."

Every year Janet selected the neediest student in her classroom and made an appointment to take him or her out for dinner at one of the finest restaurants in town. Before going to dinner, Janet took the child shopping for a new outfit. Janet has a God-given gift for building self-esteem in children.

By human standards, Janet should have been a dropout. Fear of facing an unknown future and anxiety over making wrong choices could have immobilized her. She had no father and no hope for getting her education funded. Most of us would have said, "I quit."

Had I been in Janet's position, my story might have been very different than hers. If my *triggering event* had been an alcoholic, absentee father, my *reactive emotion* would have been fear, first of all for my daily needs. Later, the fear of getting trapped in a situation similar to my mother's would have been all-consuming. I'm sure my sense of *powerlessness* would have been overwhelming—no money, no dad, no visible opportunities for a positive change in my circumstances. With my focus on how little I could do to change my situation, it would not have taken me long to move to *rage* and begin venting my anger, probably in subliminal ways first. I would have been furious with God for allowing my life to be so difficult.

With my self-reliant tendencies, my *internal negotiating* would probably have led to a destructive, rigid resolution of denial, defeat, bitterness, or escape.

But Janet selected a different course of action. I never observed her in the process, but because I saw the end result of a life based on faith-filled decisions, I wonder if she went through a process much like this.

Sorrow: I'm sure there was a day when Janet grieved over her losses. Other girls had fathers who loved them and applauded their successes. She did not. Others had bigger houses and no fear of financial hardship. Not Janet. Others had fathers with a deep faith in God who provided strong spiritual leadership. Her friends would have a loving father walk them down the aisle on their wedding day. But Janet had none of those basics.

When the deep sadness of lost opportunity hits us, there is an ache in our soul. And when we are surrounded by people who appear to have everything we desire, the sting of sadness can be very deep.

As we experience the sorrow of lost opportunity, the pain can lead to brokenness before God.

"Pain" is the fundamental human predicament. No one escapes life without experiencing pain, although many become pre-occupied with attempts to alleviate it. Pain is the overriding, inexplicable condition of life . . . the touchstone of our lives. In this "trysting place" heaven and earth meet. Here we meet each other in humanity, and more important, God meets us.[6]

Brokenness: The constructive resolution of fear always brings us to a place of brokenness. Our emotional pain is deep and we long for an escape. But in time, our pain becomes a friend that brings humility before God. Instead of telling Him how to "fix" our hurts, we say, "God, You are in charge. I'm tired. I'm hurt. I will quit trying to alleviate the problem myself. I need You."

Surrender: It's difficult to determine the exact point where brokenness turns into surrender, because a broken heart before God moves to surrender very naturally. For Janet, surrender meant giving up fantasies about "the easy life." It meant experiencing the all-encompassing love of her heavenly Father and releasing resentment. Surrender meant trusting God without knowing the answers to all of her questions.

Faith-filled decision: I wish I could invite everyone reading this book to a lunch with Janet, because you would be filled with hope. You'd leave encouraged. You would feel valued and loved. You would know you have a personal mission in this world that is different than any other woman alive. You would soon understand that you don't have to be afraid of getting trapped in a dead-end situation, no matter what your lost opportunities have been. You would know it's possible to grieve deeply over your losses and experience brokenness before God without shame. You would be convinced that God can change the future generations because Jesus lives.

You would learn how to make faith-filled decisions in the process of listening to her talk about daily life. You would have to remind yourself that the gracious, attractive, dynamic, magnetic educator before you is the product of a broken home and an alcoholic, absentee father.

Her love for children and belief in God's future potential in each of them would convince you that past fears do not have to place dark shadows over the future. Your faith would increase. You would know it is possible to overcome huge personal obstacles and your own personal fear monster.

✍ JANET'S LEGACY

Janet made many faith-filled decisions. I've listed some of them below:

- Instead of getting bitter over life without a dad, she encouraged her hardworking mother in unique, creative ways.
- Rather than being defeated in her spiritual life, she surrounded herself with Christian friends and families who provided encouragement and wise counsel.
- Instead of expecting all men to be like her father, she chose to marry and defeat the negative statistical odds about her potential marital success.
- Unlike her peers with similar backgrounds, she worked hard to pay for a university education so she could positively impact the lives of kids with difficult home situations.
- After teaching for several years, Janet became a school principal, and she is currently inspiring other educators to make a positive difference in the lives of their students.
- Through the years, Janet made *me*—her old best friend from high school—a prayer project. Janet phones and writes regularly, letting me know that she believes in what God is doing through my life and ministry.

That *is* Janet's story. But it's far more than the story of a girl from the wrong side of the tracks who had an alcoholic father and many seemingly impossible challenges in her life. It's the story of one woman who said, "I will not let the fear of getting trapped in life paralyze me. I will not live with the ghost of lost opportunity leering over my shoulder. I will believe there is a constructive resolution to fear. I believe my focus can be on God and my future with Him in a better place, rather than on myself and my personal misery. I know God can change the future generations in my family."

Instead of choosing self-reliance as a way of coping—which might have driven Janet to a life of compulsive/addictive behaviors—she chose to grieve over the sadness in her life, which led to brokenness, surrender, and a lifetime of faith-filled decisions. Her consistent example has inspired me to be a woman with a passion for God.

⁄3 CURING THE "IF ONLY" SYNDROME

It's possible to spend most of our lives looking back at the mistakes we might have made or at the opportunities that never appeared or the will of God that we think we missed. We can spend our days filling the pauses between sentences with "If only. . . . " The choice is ours.

Barbara Johnson says it well:

> IF ONLY can fill your stomach with ulcers.
>
> IF ONLY can give you high blood pressure.
>
> IF ONLY can deprive you of fun in your profession.
>
> IF ONLY can take the zing out of your marriage.
>
> IF ONLY can depress you to the point of suicide.
>
> You see, yesterday is gone forever and tomorrow may never come. TODAY IS IT! So give it your best shot, and at the end of the road you will be at the place of your choice instead of being haunted by IF ONLY, IF ONLY, IF ONLY.[7]

The fear of making wrong choices has a thousand different faces. For some, it's a lifetime of looking in the rearview mirror. For others, it's bondage to a past that convinces us there is no way to escape unhappy and unproductive choices. It can be the fear of not being able to undo past mistakes. It can involve regrets based on low self-esteem that keep us from believing God has a meaningful future for our lives.

It all boils down to the fact that we want to make choices that affirm a meaningful life.

We are obsessed with the fear of getting trapped in the "no-outlet" alleys of life, and we certainly don't want to miss out on opportunities that were designed to bring fulfillment to our lives.

My big obstacle was the fear of missing out on God's perfect will and having to settle for the dreaded "second best." As I matured and sought wise counsel, I began to find the hidden dangers in my "dot in the center of God's will" theology.

I soon ascertained that New Testament examples pointed out that direct, supernatural guidance for specific decisions was the *exception* to the general rule in Scripture. Further study helped me to see that direct guidance was given to people who played a strategic role in the drama of world evangelization and that direct guidance was provided only at critical points during the formative years of the church. My investigation further led me to understand that this direct guidance was always communicated by means of supernatural revelation.[8]

For a while it was hard to give up my cherished convictions. But I soon discovered a far better alternative. I went back to the same verses I had memorized in my youth: "I will instruct thee and teach thee in the way which thou shalt go; I will guide thee with mine eye" (Psalm 32:8, KJV). I turned to another passage, and my eyes fell on these now familiar words: "Trust GOD from the bottom of your heart; don't try to figure out everything on your own. Listen for GOD's voice in everything you do, everywhere you go; he's the one who will keep you on track" (Proverbs 3:5-6).

For the first time, instead of seeing a rigid, unyielding "only-perfect-plan-for-my-life" kind of option, I understood a truth discovered by someone else:

> God took humankind very seriously when He gave us the gift of choice; perhaps more seriously than we take ourselves. We frequently and almost carelessly . . . abdicate our autonomy and let the community, the government, or the church decide for us.[9]

I finally realized that every day, for the rest of my life, I will be making choices. Some of them will determine major courses of action; others will involve shorter blocks of time. God has given me His Word as a guide, and as I apply my heart to obeying biblical principles and as I pray for wisdom, the "straight path" He has for me will become obvious.

I had been making myself miserable with the fear of making wrong choices. Gordon Graham describes my internal conflict: "Decision is a sharp knife that cuts clean and straight; indecision is a dull one that hacks and tears and leaves ragged edges behind it."[10] My second thoughts about God's will constantly left me with confusion, indecision, and a "hacked-off" edge on my attitude.

I began to realize that God was not playing a cruel game up in heaven, making Christians guess which path they should be on. He gave us very specific direction about being people of integrity, honesty, and commitment. For the first time, I read Scripture with a sense of release, instead of seeing my life choices based on inflexible rules and regulations. I read, "Skilled living gets its start in the Fear-of-GOD, insight into life from knowing a Holy God" (Proverbs 9:10). and "Put GOD in charge of your work, then what you've planned will take place" (Proverbs 16:3). Another principle seized my attention: "wise men and women listen to each other's counsel" (Proverbs 13:10).

It was freeing to base my choices on my knowledge of God's character and His Word. As I prayed for guidance related to major decisions, I looked for individuals who were capable of offering wise counsel. I asked God to put a "check" in my spirit if I was headed in a direction that was inappropriate.

This new liberty was an exciting adventure. Instead of being filled with anxiety over the past "if onlys" or my present trap of circumstances or my lost opportunities of the future, I was experiencing a desire to dedicate my potential to Him. I realized that in former days my paralyzing fear had often led to a destructive resolution of escaping into a fog of indecision and then expecting God to come through for me with a lightning bolt of insight or a neon sign in the sky. As I learned to yield to Him with a heart attitude of humility and surrender, faith-filled decisions—even on the tough issues of life—became a natural outgrowth of a dynamic and growing relationship with Him.

The process felt risky at first. I kept looking for those well-marked road signs and God's voice through a megaphone. But I made progress. My faith grew. Instead of fearing the journey, I was learning to fear God with an awesome respect I had not known. Courage replaced hesitation. Insecurities were exchanged for confidence. I knew I could never go back to my old fears. The future was filled with opportunities. The prospects for serving Him were limitless. Godly wisdom would allow me to make the hard choices. This new lifestyle brought a peace I had not known before. And one day I knew something was missing—my lifelong fear of making wrong choices.

Elizabeth Dole summarizes what it took me so long to learn:

> It is not what I do that matters, but what a sovereign God
> chooses to do through me. God doesn't want worldly successes.
> He wants me. He wants my heart in submission to Him. Life is
> not just a few years to spend on self-indulgence and career

advancement. It's a privilege, a responsibility, a stewardship to be lived according to a much higher calling—God's calling. This alone gives true meaning to life.[11]

Janet learned the secret. No blaming the past. No paralyzing anxieties about the future.

Walk through open doors and do what your hand finds to do with all your might! Touch some lives along the way. Forgive as you've been forgiven. Hold your head high. Laugh hard. Show compassion. Love passionately. Let go of fear. Life on earth doesn't get better than that!

"WHAT IF REACHING MY GOALS ISN'T ENOUGH?"

Fear 10: Achieving Success/Admitting Failure

Biographies of bold disciples begin with chapters of honest terror. Fear of death. Fear of failure. Fear of loneliness. Fear of a wasted life. . . . Faith begins when you see God on the mountain and you are in the valley and you know that you're too weak to make the climb. You see what you need . . . you see what you have . . . and it isn't enough . . . but He is! . . . Faith that begins with fear will end up nearer the Father.

MAX LUCADO
In the Eye of the Storm

My stormy emotions are in sharp contrast to the sunshine outside. I've been trying to swallow the lump in my throat since early this morning. Why am I fighting back tears when I should be celebrating? My mind is playing back the recording of almost two decades of time—and I've been pausing to remember significant events, places, milestones, challenges, and laughs—a lot of laughs. The playback simultaneously brings exhilarating joy and unbearable pain. I feel fearful and weak. An important era of my life is ending in a few days.

The call came from the congressman's office: "Congratulations! Jason Paul Kent has been awarded an appointment to the U.S. Naval Academy. If he accepts the appointment, he'll be heading for Annapolis soon. Mrs. Kent, you have an extraordinary son. You must be very proud of him."

I was proud, all right. The competition had been fierce. The interviews were long. And the paperwork was endless. I made appropriate remarks to the district liaison, put the phone down, and faced reality as my tears flowed shamelessly. My son was headed for a military career. My baby was leaving home very shortly. The child of my womb was saying yes to an unknown future and would never return home in quite the same way that he had in the previous eighteen years. My nest would be empty. My "fear of something that hadn't happened yet" was becoming a reality!

13 RUNNING THE TAPE

Mental flashbacks took me to his first day of school and on to the first time he was allowed to ride his two-wheeler on the street. I thought about our hot, week-long car trip to visit the Grand Canyon and of our mission trip to Mexico. I remembered the day he came home from school with tears in his eyes because he was shunned by fellow students for being the only one on his row who refused to participate in a cheating scam during math class.

Then I recalled the day shortly before his fifth birthday when I was helping him memorize Romans 6:23. He looked up quizzically and said, "Mom, what are the wages of sin?" That was the day he asked Jesus to be his personal Savior.

In addition to the high points, which were many, there were challenges.

Dirty laundry. Lots of dirty laundry. A messy room. Questionable posters. Testing limits. Confrontations. A few tears. Setting guidelines. Learning to let go. Taking back authority. Overreacting. Apologizing. Forgiving. Laughing. Loving. How could eighteen years have ended so abruptly?

⅏ EVALUATING SUCCESS

Each of us comes to specific crossroads in life when we stop and ask ourselves if we are achieving the success we so desperately want. I'm at one of those junctions of introspection right now. And for most of my lifetime I've had a tough time judging whether or not I'm succeeding or failing. And I'm so afraid of failing!

My mind went back to an incident I first shared in *Speak Up With Confidence:*

> I had jumped out of bed early, showered, dressed hurriedly, and sat reading the paper at the kitchen table while enjoying a freshly brewed cup of coffee.
>
> J.P. (Jason Paul) came downstairs a few minutes later. I made him some breakfast and returned to my coffee. Minutes later while peering at me over his cereal bowl, he said, "Mama, you look so pretty today."
>
> I couldn't believe it. On most days I'm quite dressed up— always a bit more comfortable in a suit and heels than in a pair of blue jeans and sneakers. On the day in question, I had dressed for leisure—nothing special, just slacks and a sweater.
>
> We made eye contact, and I questioned him: "Honey, why do you think I look pretty today? These are old clothes, and usually Mother's wearing something nicer."

He flashed his gorgeous blue eyes and smiled at me. "It's because," he said thoughtfully, "when you're all dressed up, I know you're going out some place, but when you look like this, I know you're all mine!"

His answer was like an arrow, piercing my heart and pinning me to the back of the chair. It had never dawned on me that this little boy could tell if I had *time* for him by what I was wearing on any given day.[1]

It was at that time in my life when I faced the fear of becoming a failure at the one thing I most wanted to succeed at—motherhood. New choices were necessary, but in the middle of my fear of failure, I did not know how to begin making faith-filled decisions that would redirect my priorities.

13 THE GREAT PARADOX: FEARING SUCCESS AND FAILURE

As we grapple with the fear of making wrong choices, we make a surprising discovery. If we achieve the success we think we desire, we may have difficult decisions and time constraints that require sacrifices. Fear builds as we give months and years to organizations, companies, and even churches—but we're not sure we've spent our energy on the most important goals. Erwin Lutzer once said, "Many who are climbing the ladder of success have their ladders leaning against the wrong walls."[2]

Triggering situation: Most of us experience a sense of elation when we finally find our niche in life. I've always believed that success is finding out what God wants us to do with our uniqueness and then doing it with all our might. The problem comes when we enjoy our work/ministry so much that it begins to take over every area of our lives. In my case, a growing ministry was demanding more days away from home and more preoccupation at home while I answered mail and returned phone calls.

The situation that triggered my fear went right back to undefined priorities. I had never taken the time to decide what was most important to me, so I let phone calls, aggressive meeting planners, urgent demands, and ministry preparation keep me so busy I never thought about saying "no" and choosing a more relaxed schedule. In the beginning I was having fun. I was in demand. I enjoyed having the acclaim of "doing it all." And I felt spiritual. After all, I was doing God's work—at least I'd convinced myself that this move into overcommitment was for Him.

Reactive emotion: It didn't take long for me to begin fearing success and failure at the same time. The more successful I became, the more time demands were placed on my schedule. And the more I began writing books and accepting speaking engagements, the less time I had to be an at-home mother. I was afraid of success because I didn't know how to set limits. I was also afraid of failure, because in my mind, if I hurt my child by being too busy, no other form of success could make up for that type of failure. This monster fear began preoccupying my mind and produced tremendous guilt.

Rage: I experienced an inner boiling cauldron of rage, and it was often directed at different people. During the times I lived through an impossible schedule, I was furious with myself. I would return home in the middle of the night from the airport, tiptoe into my son's bedroom, pray over his sleeping figure—and realize I had just missed three days of his life.

At other times I would walk into a room and see my husband reading a good book or playing a game with Jason and a surge of anger would envelop me. I was filled with rage as I saw Gene with extra hours to enjoy reading and being a father. I wanted the same freedom and privilege—but my schedule was so full I rarely had time for those personal luxuries.

Internal negotiating: Living every day in the middle of rage is so uncomfortable that we usually move to internal negotiating. I had to ask myself why my husband's legitimate and wise use of his leisure time made me so angry. It was hard for me to admit I resented him because he had chosen what I wanted—time for Jason and time to breathe.

Destructive solutions: I had great coping skills, so my internal negotiations immediately turned to finding a resolution for my fear of failure. At different times, I tried each of the following resolutions.

1. *Denial*—I convinced myself that I always spent "quality time" with my son, and that's what mattered. He was doing well in school and had a very involved father. I was only making myself guilty and fearful because of a silly self-imposed standard of excellence that no parent could ever live up to.

2. *Defeat*—Exhaustion is the constant companion of women who don't set limits, and when I was tired, I threw personal pity parties. I was smiling on the outside, but inside I was convinced that my worst fear had come true—I was a rotten mother. In fact, I was a screaming mother, an irritated wife, and an agitated human being. Phone calls, e-mail, and interruptions overwhelmed me. I started to prove to myself and my family that I was a failure! I was too tired to entertain company at home. I certainly could not work as hard as I did and be an energized bed partner with my husband. I could not cook well-rounded, nutritious meals while simultaneously keeping the house in impeccable condition. My mother *always* had a clean house and cooked big dinners. I was a failure, and I was defeated!

3. *Bitterness*—I never experienced an extended period of bitterness, but I remember "seasons of embitterment." The year I missed all but two Little League games was the time bitterness hit me in the face. We had experienced some financial challenges that year, and I was realizing that my income had become a necessary part of meeting our monthly obligations. In the beginning I had worked hard because I enjoyed it. Now I was working even harder because we needed the money to meet our financial commitments.

Bitterness always looks for someone or something to blame, and my mind was great at creating a list to fault others:

- If my husband would work harder and make more money, I wouldn't have to be on the road so much.
- If the Little League committee had an ounce of compassion, they'd schedule the games when I could come.
- If we hadn't bought this house, I wouldn't have to work so hard and I could spend more time with my son.
- If God really cared about me, He would give me back the joy I lost.

Bitterness is a debilitating choice. It always poisons *us* more than it contaminates those we blame.

4. *Escape*—My fear of failing as a mother was closely tied to my fear of losing control. For a while, I found myself sinking deeply in the compulsive addictions of work and perfectionism. I was miserably unhappy, and my fear of failure loomed in the background, reminding me that success had a price tag.

⅓ WIDENING THE SCOPE OF A SECRET FEAR

I have never met a woman who has not struggled at some level with the fear of success or the fear of failure. One woman wrote, "I have desperately wanted everyone, anyone, or someone to think I was wonderful, talented, exciting, and spiritual. But I have been so afraid of failure that I have turned off my ability to accept success as well." This woman's self-esteem was so fragile due to past issues that she was in bondage to the fear of failure.

On the other hand, some of us are overwhelmed by the secret fear that to be successful, we must do something so spectacular that the whole world will validate our worth. When we get caught up in this philosophy, we often *do* accomplish something worthy of applause, but often the fear of failure looms in the background because of the personal sacrifices that have allowed the success.

Helen Keller once said, "I long to accomplish a great and noble task; but it is my chief duty and joy to accomplish humble tasks as though they were great and noble. The world is moved along, not only by the mighty shoves of its heroes, but also by the aggregate of the tiny pushes of each honest worker."[3] I've struggled with exactly what Helen Keller talked about. Why did I always feel more successful when I was doing what felt like "important work" than when I was doing laundry for my family or making peanut butter sandwiches for Jason and his friends? Sometimes I think one of life's most important challenges is to understand the value of humble tasks. We are so afraid that being "ordinary" and taking time to relax means we are not successful.

This last fear is a giant force in most of our lives. As women who desire to achieve greatness and accomplish worthy deeds for God, we face many fearful challenges. A few of the fears women have shared with me follow:

- I'm afraid I'll be looked at as less competent if I don't work through my lunch hour. I have to work harder all the time to outdo the competition.
- I'm afraid to get more education even though I'm unhappy in my job. What if I'm not smart enough to get decent grades?
- I'm afraid to have a child because I might not be a good enough mother.
- I'm very unhappy in my current position, but I'm afraid to try something new because I might not be successful.
- I'm afraid to approach my boss about a raise because I might be turned down, and I'd feel like a total failure.

- I'm afraid to accept the chairmanship of the organization because I might not have the skills to be successful.
- I'm afraid to get married to this man because he might be disappointed in me, and I couldn't risk that.
- What if I work hard for my entire life and discover I'm still empty inside?

Much of our fear centers on being unable to identify what will bring a sense of purpose, joy, and fulfillment to our lives. Fear of making the wrong choice in our life's work. Fear of getting trapped in dead-end marriages and/or vocations. Fear of *not* having children. Fear of *having* children and being bad parents. Fear of not knowing how to handle success. Fear of not feeling fulfilled when everyone says we are successful. Fear of trying something new because we've never succeeded in the past.

David Frähm wrote,

If you don't dream your own dreams, others will project their dreams onto you. Then your direction will be by default, not by choice. The only real direction you'll be headed in is around in circles. . . . The Christian who lacks a sense of personal vision for her work, who has yet to clarify the mental picture of what she'd like to do in her world, lacks passion and purpose. Her work life will feel more like purgatory than a privileged cooperation with the One who made her.[4]

As we try to break out of bondage and tame the fear monster, we will always experience some failures along the way. To dream our own dreams means to risk failing more than once. It means developing a constructive resolution for the way we process fear. As we develop the ability to arrive at faith-filled decisions instead of being paralyzed by our fears of success and failure, we discover that every successful person we know has gotten where they are by learning how to process their failure feelings in a constructive way.

⅍ REMEMBERING FEARS OF THE PAST

We've looked at five major areas of fear in this book. I've come through many of them—but I'm still in the process of facing others. Dealing with lifelong fear is a dynamic process of choosing to face the fear, acknowledging the pain, and implementing a constructive resolution. Here's a quick reminder of those five major fears.

THE FEAR OF THINGS THAT HAVEN'T HAPPENED ... YET!

Engraved on my mind is a list of the paralyzing phobias that have at times kept me frozen in a state of inactivity. Sometimes when I dwell on the events of September 11, I feel frozen in my fear. Terrible things can happen to anyone at any time. But then I look back at the huge list of the potential disasters I have been sure would happen. I chuckle when I realize that more than half of the dreaded possibilities never took place, but I feel sad when I'm reminded of all my wasted mental and spiritual energy—energy that could have been invested in something productive!

THE FEAR OF BEING VULNERABLE

This fear haunts me the most, because at times, I still feel more secure when I'm "in control" of people and events, instead of letting people get close enough to share my personal hurts and failings. As I daily choose to reveal myself without debilitating anxiety about what people will think of me, I take a step in the right direction.

The Fear of Abandonment

Some of us are plagued by the fear of disappointing people. Even though old patterns tempt us, it's encouraging to see ourselves leaving codependency behind and allowing the people around us to be responsible for their own actions. The fear of abandonment may occasionally tempt us with thoughts of insecurity. But every time we face rejection, we can choose to allow the pain to draw us closer to God. Instead of feeling trapped in our pain, we can choose a constructive resolution to this fear.

The Fear of Truth

Lloyd Douglas once said, "If a man harbors any kind of fear, it makes him landlord to a ghost." Looking back is often painful, and if there has been severe emotional, physical, or spiritual abuse, we've faced two ghosts—shame and guilt. The shame of victimization can be brutal, but sometimes the guilt for the wrong choices we've made is even worse—until we understand the power of forgiveness. When life brings disappointments that jolt our confidence in God, we have a decision to make. We can wind up defeated and bitter, or our brokenness can lead to surrender and a future based on a faith-filled decision to forgive ourselves and others.

The Fear of Making Wrong Choices

A few years ago a friend sent me a cartoon of a woman who came to a fork in the road and wound up crashing into a pole in between the two choices. As she stumbled out of her car with blurred vision, broken bones, and open wounds, she said, "I just couldn't decide which way to go."

This book is all about choices. Will we be consumed with the fear of getting trapped in the "dead ends" of life? Will we be afraid of success because of the hard decisions we'll have to make and the personal limitations we'll have to face? Will we allow the fear of failure to keep us from trying to achieve? Or will we use the events and situations that trigger our fears to move us toward faith-filled decisions? It inspires me to know that I have a choice—every day. It's the daily choices that produce lifetime results.

13 THE VALUE OF FAILURE

When we allow our internal negotiation to lead us to a constructive resolution for our fears, we get a new perspective on the value of failure. Christian psychologist and author H. Norman Wright says,

> You have failed in the past. You are failing now in some way. You
> will fail in the future. You weren't perfect in the past. You won't
> be perfect in the future. Your children will not be perfect, either.
> When you fail, allow yourself to feel disappointment, but not
> disapproval. . . . You can fail and not be a failure![5]

In other words, failure's positive contribution to my life is that it leads me to explore the depth of my disappointment, which has the potential of bringing me to a place of personal and spiritual growth. Instead of covering up my fear with denial, beating myself up with defeat, picking victims for my bitterness, or selecting an escape into a compulsive/addictive pattern, I can allow failure to launch me in a different direction.

I think the apostle Paul understood this concept.

> I've got my eye on the goal, where God is beckoning us
> onward—to Jesus. I'm off and running, and I'm not turning back.
> So let's keep focused on that goal, those of us who want every-
> thing God has for us. (Philippians 3:13-14)

✍ LESSONS LEARNED THE HARD WAY

Thinking back on my life brings a realization of the tension in my heart as I have battled the fear of success and failure throughout much of my life. It would be absolutely wrong for me to suggest that on a certain day I learned how to practice a constructive resolution for that fear and I never had a problem with it again. Many times I fell back into old patterns and had to make new choices. But, in time, I have learned how to come to a constructive resolution faster. And I've also learned how miserable I am when I go back into my "I'll-take-care-of-the-problem-myself" mode. It just doesn't work! So what *does* work?

Sorrow: When I allow my fears to bring me to a place of grieving, I've already begun to "give up my rights," and I've started to release my tenacious grip on the situation. As a young mother, I grieved for the time I had lost with my child because of overcommitment. I wept for the false guilt I had placed on my husband for not being as committed to his work as I was. I lamented over my own total inability to know how to relax.

Brokenness: This sorrow led to a brokenness I had never experienced before. Instead of figuring out how God could fix a situation and giving Him all of the multiple-choice options I had constructed, I said, "Lord, I'm hurting. I'm broken. I'm a failure as a wife and a mother. I'm a phony Christian leader, and I'm at the end of my resources. None of the successes I've had mean anything to me, because they have not brought happiness. I cannot go on like this."

Surrender: For me, surrender meant getting on my knees with my precious date book in my hand and offering it to God. That book represented everything that made me feel important. It also represented the birthdays of significant people in my life, an anniversary with my husband, family vacations, and lunch dates with friends who were wondering if I cared about them anymore. I confessed my self-reliance to God, admitting that I had allowed urgencies and personal pride to crowd out the important things in my life. I wanted to learn how to be successful by God's standards.

Faith-filled decision: Out of the yielding pattern of sorrow, brokenness, and surrender comes an empowerment that sets us free from fear. Instead of being in bondage to indecision, we have a supernatural strength to make wise choices. Paul said it best: "God doesn't want us to be shy with his gifts, but bold and loving and sensible" (2 Timothy 1:7).

As I surrendered my calendar, my plans, my ego, and my insecurities to God, I experienced a new understanding of success. I was able to make the hard choices more easily and form the words, "Thanks for asking, but I'm not available," with greater authority and joy. I moved to a new plan for defining my priorities. I saved days on the calendar ahead of time—just for our family—before making them available to the first person who called.

When my focus was on God, instead of me, self-reliance was relinquished and I was infused with a joy and personal relaxation I forgot was possible. I was no longer afraid of success, because I had a new definition of it. I was no longer afraid of failing as a mother. I had *time* to *be* a mother.

I rediscovered the truth of Isaiah 41:9-10,13:

"You're my servant, serving on my side.
I've picked you. I haven't dropped you.
Don't panic. I'm with you.
There's no need to fear for I'm your God.
I'll give you strength. I'll help you.
I'll hold you steady, keep a firm grip on you. . .
Don't panic. I'm right here to help you."

Fear is energy-draining. The surrender that leads to faith-filled decision making is energizing and freeing.

✍ FAITH OR FEAR?

The opposite of fear is faith. Fear makes us withdraw and hide behind our escape mechanisms. Fear exposes our disappointments and makes us choose a rigid or a yielding resolution for those fears. Faith or fear? The choice is ours.

Bruce Larson says, "Fear is a handle for laying hold on God. When you stop running and face your fear head on with faith, you find God. It is His presence and power that move us beyond our fears—past, present, and future."[6]

Sometimes faith feels risky and fear seems like a comfortable burden. What will we choose? Reva Nelson, the author of a book on risk taking, describes the kind of risk that leads to faith: "to decide to take action, beyond your usual limitations, for a vision, when the results are not guaranteed, but look positive." Every day I have a choice. Will I allow fear to overcome me, or will I take action, even though the results are not guaranteed, and look with faith into the face of my Savior?

The events of September 11 have forever changed our lives. What will life be like for our children and our grandchildren? Will we give in to the bondage of past fears—or will we be set free to make new goals, dream new dreams, and use today's opportunities to make a positive difference in God's kingdom? Will you join me in this prayer?

Lord, give me the grace to realize life on this earth will never be completely free from anxiety. I know the enemy will harass me with fear for the future and with memories of past failures and I will be tempted to fall back into old patterns of handling my fears.

Protect me from the bondage of denial and defeat. Guard my heart from the cancer of bitterness. Keep me from my favorite escapes into perfectionism and workaholism.

Lord, when fear surfaces, help me to grieve over the pain

without shame and let my broken heart turn me to humble surrender and forgiveness. Enable me to practice making faith-filled decisions as I submit to Your authority in my life. Keep me from demanding instant answers and help me to understand the simple truth: *Faith that begins with fear will end up closer to You.* Amen.

TWELVE-WEEK BIBLE STUDY

WEEK I

Read Chapter 1, "If I'm Such a Great Christian, Why Do I Have This Problem?"

Warm-up: If you are meeting with a group, give your name and then describe the room in your house or apartment where you feel the most peaceful, safe, and relaxed. Share why you enjoy spending time there.

1. Memorize Psalm 27:1 (NIV). Write it out on a 3 x 5 card and carry it with you this week. Rehearse the verse while you are in the car running errands. Tape a copy to your bathroom mirror. If you're meeting with a group, read the verse aloud together: "The LORD is my light and my salvation—whom shall I fear? The LORD is the stronghold of my life—of whom shall I be afraid?"

   a. Why do you think there are so many references to overcoming fear in the Bible?

   b. Describe what it means to you to know the Lord is your light and the stronghold of your life.

2. In your own words, how do you define the word *fear*?

3. How would you rate your struggle with fear on a scale of 1 to 10?
One means, "fear is not a problem for me, and it never has been."
Ten means, "I've struggled with fear for most of my life, and at
times it paralyzes me."

1	2	3	4	5	6	7	8	9	10

Freedom from Fear   Paralyzing Fear Problem

4. Read the background information on the three types of fear on
page 16 and describe the following:

   a. Holy fear

   b. Self-preserving fear

   c. Slavish fear

5. Genesis 3:10 (NIV) quotes Adam saying, "I heard you in the garden, and I was afraid because I was naked; so I hid." It's been said
that the negative aspect of fear is a problem of (1) focus and (2)
self-reliance. How does the story of Adam in the Garden of Eden
demonstrate the truth of that statement? (See page 16.)

6. Proverbs 28:1 says, "The wicked are edgy with guilt, ready to run
off even when no one's after them; Honest people are relaxed and
confident, bold as lions."

   a. Why do you think fear often causes us to run and hide?

b. When you encounter fearful situations, do you seek a quiet place where you can actually be alone physically, or are you more likely to hide emotionally from the people you are close to?

7. Read the section in the book called "A Positive Side to Fear?" on pages 19. Describe a time when fear moved you toward positive action, appropriate power, and the energy to do your best in a new situation.

8. Chapter 1 discusses five forms of fear. Read the descriptions on pages 20-25. Which of the following forms of fear is the most difficult for you to deal with during this season of your life? Why?

☐ The Fear of Things That Haven't Happened . . . Yet!
☐ The Fear of Being Vulnerable
☐ The Fear of Abandonment
☐ The Fear of Truth
☐ The Fear of Making Wrong Choices

9. Answer the following questions on your own this week:

☐ Are my fears the same as fears faced by other women?
☐ Can fear be controlled?
☐ Is my perfectionism actually based in the fear of being vulnerable?
☐ If I reveal myself to you, will you accept me—or judge me?
☐ Why am I afraid that the worst-case scenario will happen to me or to my family?
☐ Why am I so afraid of being rejected, abandoned, or lonely?

□ If I face the fears of the past and admit the truth, will I cause
myself more pain?

□ Can I really be a Christian if I struggle with fear?

□ Is there a positive side to fear that could actually be a springboard to success and happiness?

10. First John 4:18-19 says, "There is no room in love for fear. Well-
formed love banishes fear. Since fear is crippling, a fearful
life. . . is one not yet fully formed in love."

a. Why do you think well-formed love eliminates fear?

b. What one thing will you do to demonstrate your love to a
fearful person this week?

WEEK 2

Read Chapter 2, "What Happens Inside My Head When I'm Afraid?"

1. Where were you on September 11, 2001, when you heard that
two planes had crashed into the World Trade Center? What was
your initial response?

2. Memorize 2 Timothy 1:7 (NIV). "For God did not give us a spirit of
timidity, but a spirit of power, of love and of self-discipline." If
you're meeting with a group, say the verse aloud together. Write
this verse on a Post-It note or on a 3 x 5 card and carry it with you.
Review the verse when you have a few extra minutes each day.

a. Who do you know who lives out a positive example of having "a spirit of power, of love and of self-discipline?" Explain.

b. Can you describe a time in your life when God turned your timidity into boldness?

There's a chain reaction all of us go through when we face fear. Here's what we experience:

Triggering Event, Situation, or Person

⇩

Reactive Emotion

⇩

Powerlessness

⇩

Rage

⇩

Internal Negotiating

3. There is always a trigger point that makes us aware of danger, evil, or pain. The cause might be from a real or imagined source, but it feels threatening, harmful, and disarming. What "trigger points" produce a fearful response in you?

4. Our first honest reaction to the triggering event is virtually involuntary. It might be shock, terror, panic, dread, anxiety, horror, hurt, anger, or shame. One person might have a panic reaction that is immediately recognizable as fear. Someone else's first response might be anger, which could be displayed by a volatile

outburst or by passive, wounded withdrawal.

With your personality, what emotional response to fear are you most likely to demonstrate? Circle the descriptive words in the previous paragraph that best describe your normal reaction. Share your "key words" with the group and feel free to comment.

5. After we have (1) identified a trigger point, (2) experienced a reactive emotion, (3) felt powerless, and (4) responded with demonstrative or internal rage, we begin (5) internal negotiating. Read about the destructive courses of action on pages 38-39. Circle the destructive choice you are most likely to make in the middle of a fear-producing situation.

Denial   Defeat   Bitterness   Escape

6. Read Matthew 14:22-33.

   a. What were the uncertain circumstances the disciples faced?

   b. What wrong conclusion did they arrive at?

   c. Peter yelled out a desperate call: "Lord, save me!" Think of a time in your life when you felt that desperate. What happened?

   d. There was immediate calm because Jesus reached out to him "without delay" and said, "You of little faith . . . why did you doubt?" Why do you think many of us don't experience this immediate calming connection with God in the middle of our overwhelming fears?

7. Read the definitions of the six disguises of fear on pages 34-35. Which of the following are you the most likely to use? Please explain.

☐ A perfectionist lifestyle
☐ A possessive nature
☐ A picky attitude
☐ A pretentious faith
☐ A passionate workaholism
☐ A plastic smile

8. Read the constructive course of action for dealing with fear on pages 39-41. Write a brief description of each step below:
   a. Sorrow

   b. Brokenness

   c. Surrender

   d. Faith-filled decision

9. Identify a fear in your own life right now. Look at the four steps above that describe a positive, biblically based resolution for fear. Take some time this week to write down where you are in your journey toward making a faith-filled decision about how to handle that fear. Make an appointment with a friend and ask her to

pray with you as you complete the process of surrendering your fear issues to God.

WEEK 3
Read Chapter 3, "Why Do I Let Irrational Panic Immobilize Me?"

1. What is your earliest memory of being afraid? When you were growing up, who was the main person who calmed your fears?

2. Memorize Joshua 1:9 (NIV): "Have I not commanded you? Be strong and courageous. Do not be terrified; do not be discouraged, for the LORD your God will be with you wherever you go."
   a. Read Joshua 1:1-9. Why was Joshua feeling a lot of anxiety?

   b. Have you ever been asked to do a job that you thought was "too big" for your abilities? If so, what was your response?

3. When a triggering event produces a reactive emotion of fear that develops into an irrational panic, it is easy to feel powerless. We then move to rage and then on to internal negotiating. A few of the things we sometimes internalize and believe (at least for a while) are listed below. Place an "x" in front of any of the comments you can identify with regarding your reaction to past fears.

   ☐ "I sometimes feel totally powerless to change my fearful situation."

☐ "I know I'm supposed to trust God when I feel afraid, but that really seems like a pat 'spiritualized' answer that doesn't mean much to me."

☐ "At times I believe there is nothing I can do to alter my losing reaction to fear."

☐ "I frequently feel very angry at the person who triggers this fear in me!"

☐ "I usually refuse to dwell on my fears. If other Christians would just forget their fears and get on with their lives, they could be happy, too."

☐ "I get so mad at myself and embarrassed in front of people when I'm paralyzed by fear."

☐ "I usually wonder what God wants me to learn from the fearful situations I face."

☐ "I'm beginning to believe I can't handle my fears, and I feel like giving up on trying."

☐ "I'm convinced if I had more supportive people in my life, I'd be able to let go of my fears."

☐ "I really don't ever have a problem with fear. If I work harder and get more involved in worthy causes, I'll forget my worries."

4. Which of the above "internal responses" is most typical of your response to fear? Explain.

5. Moses experienced major fear when God called him to lead the children of Israel. Summarize the main point in each of the following verses:

a. Exodus 3:6-10

    b. Exodus 3:11

    c. Exodus 4:1

    d. Exodus 4:10

    e. Exodus 4:11-12

    f. Exodus 4:13

6. Someone once described FEAR in an acronym: "*False Expectations Appearing Real*. For the most part, what we fear is not real—it is merely our mind imagining something awful that has not yet happened."[1] Do you agree or disagree with that statement? Why?

7. Philippians 4:6-7 says, "Don't fret or worry. Instead of worrying, pray. Let petitions and praises shape your worries into prayers, letting God know your concerns. Before you know it, a sense of God's wholeness, everything coming together for good, will come and settle you down. It's wonderful what happens when Christ displaces worry at the center of your life."

    a. According to this passage, what should we do instead of worrying?

b. What benefits will follow if we heed God's instructions for dealing with anxiety?

c. Give your opinion on why we continue to choose worry over trust, even when we say we believe the Bible.

8. Think of one thing you are worried about right now. Stop now to "shape your worries into prayers." If you're meeting with a group, you may pray silently or aloud. The discussion leader can close the session in prayer.

WEEK 4
Read Chapter 4, "Why Does the Fear of Things That Might Happen Consume My Mental and Spiritual Energy?"

1. When you think about the future, do you tend to dwell on the potential best-case scenario or the worst-case scenario? Why?

2. Memorize Matthew 6:34 (NIV): "Therefore do not worry about tomorrow, for tomorrow will worry about itself. Each day has enough trouble of its own."
   a. Summarize that verse in your own words.

b. Is your typical day characterized with a lot of low-level worry and anxiety, or do you take each day as it comes without too much stress?

3. Our fears are often based on things that might happen. Place an "x" in the box next to any of the following trigger points you struggle with in your own life.

☐ "What if I lose someone I love? I don't know how I could go on without that person in my life."

☐ "What if I lose my job? The company is going to lay off more people, and I just know I'll be one of them."

☐ "What if I'm a bad mother? How can I ever be sure I'm raising my children properly? What if they turn away from God?"

☐ "What if the economy falls apart? How will we have enough money to live?"

☐ "What if the terrorists strike again? What will happen to our country?"

☐ "What if I have an accident?"

☐ "What if I can't afford to pay for my children's education? People can't make a living in today's world without a university degree."

☐ "What if I never get married?"

☐ "What if I can't get pregnant? I want a child more than anything, and every month my disappointment is deeper and I fear the worst—infertility."

☐ "What if my husband gets interested in another woman? He's so attractive and the women in his office flirt with him all the time."

☐ "What if we get transferred to another place? My whole world is wrapped up in this community. My family lives here. I have meaningful ministry in my church. I just *can't* leave here."

☐ "What if I face death prematurely? I know heaven is my final destination, but I am so afraid of the *process* of dying."

4. Which one of the previous fears have you struggled with the most? Does your imagination ever add to the fear? Share your thoughts with the group.

5. Read Luke 1:26-38. It's the story of Mary, the mother of Jesus. She was young, engaged, and in love with a wonderful man. Then the angel came with a shocking announcement. That was her *triggering event!* Summarize what happened in the following verses:

Luke 1:28

Luke 1:29

Luke 1:30-33

Luke 1:34

Luke 1:35-37

Luke 1:38

222 TWELVE-WEEK BIBLE STUDY

6. Corrie ten Boom once said: "Worry is a cycle of inefficient thoughts whirling around a center of fear. . . . Worry doesn't empty tomorrow of its sorrow; it empties today of its strength."[2] Do you agree or disagree with this statement? Why?

7. Review the "Five Simple Truths" on pages 66-68. At this stage of your life, which one is the most important to you? Explain.

8. This week write a letter of thanks or send an e-mail note to someone in your life who has helped you to overcome a troublesome fear, or to someone who has encouraged you during a fearful time in your life.

WEEK 5
Read Chapter 5, "Why Does Everything I Do Have to Be Perfect?"

1. Where were you in the birth order of your family?

   a. Did you "boss" siblings, or were you "bossed?"

   b. In what ways do you think your position in the birth order affected the types of fears you have experienced as an adult?

2. Memorize Matthew 11:28-30: "Are you tired? Worn out? Burned out on religion? Come to me. Get away with me and you'll recover your life. I'll show you how to take a real rest. Walk with

me and work with me—watch how I do it. Learn the unforced rhythms of grace. I won't lay anything heavy or ill-fitting on you. Keep company with me and you'll learn to live freely and lightly."

    a. Where do you currently feel the most "burdened" in your life?

    b. When in your life have you experienced the unforced rhythms of grace?

3. Taking control is burdensome work! Barbara Sullivan says, "Control is an outgrowth of fear, insecurity, and lack of self-esteem. The more anxious a woman is the more she wants to control and, conversely, the more secure a woman is the less likely she will need to control."[3]

Do you agree or disagree with that statement. Why?

4. On the following scale, circle the number that best represents how controlling you are. If you're meeting with a group, you can share the number you circled.

1   2   3   4   5   6   7   8   9   10
I dislike controlling others.   I like to be in charge.

5. The fear of losing control wears a variety of disguises. Read through the descriptions on pages 80-83 and place a check in front of any of the ten controlling identities you sometimes assume:

    ☐ The Manager
    ☐ The Manipulator

☐ The Martyr

☐ The Meanie

☐ The Most Spiritual

☐ The Mother of the Extended Family

☐ The Most Perfect Person

☐ The Mime

☐ The Morbid Weakling

☐ The Main Attraction

Share with your group the controlling disguise you wear most often.

6. Look at a few controlling women in the Bible and see if you can identify which of the ten disguises described above fit each one. In some cases, there may be more than one correct response:

    a. Rebekah (Genesis 25:21-28; 27:1-10)

    b. Delilah (Judges 16)

    c. Jezebel (1 Kings 21:1-15)

    d. Martha (Luke 10:38-40)

7. Paul was one of the most gifted leaders of all time. He was a powerful speaker, a seasoned missionary, a survivor of torture, and a man of great influence. If anyone was ever tempted to see the benefits of control, it had to be Paul.

a. Why do you think he said, "For when I am weak, then I am strong"(2 Corinthians 12:10, NIV)?

b. What application does that statement have for your own life?

8. If you're meeting with a group, pair up with one or two other people for this exercise. If you're on your own, write down your answers and consider telling one friend what you've learned about yourself.

a. Read through the warning signs on pages 85-86 and mark your "yes" responses.

b. Tell as much as you feel comfortable with about a fear you are currently experiencing.

c. How do you feel about your significance to God right now?

d. Have you been a controlling woman in the past? Do you have any sin to confess? (Remember, the constructive resolution for dealing with the fear of losing control is through *sorrow*, *brokenness*, and *surrender*, which bring you to the place of being able to make *faith-filled decisions*.)

e. Spend some time praying for each other. Commit to keeping what is shared confidential.

WEEK 6
Read Chapter 6, "If I Let You Get Close to Me, Will You Still Like Me?"

1. Do you ever feel fearful when meeting new people? Do you prefer the safety of being with people who've known you for a long time? If your answer to either of these questions is yes, what goes through your mind when you're with new people?

2. Memorize 1 John 4:18 (NIV). "There is no fear in love. But perfect love drives out fear."

    a. According to this verse, what is the opposite of fear?

    b. Why do you think perfect love has the power to get rid of fear in a relationship?

3. Webster's says the "vulnerable" person is "open to attack, hurt or injury; [capable] of being. . . wounded [either because of being insufficiently protected or because of being sensitive and tender]; liable to greater penalties than the opponents."[4]

    a. Do you have at least one friend with whom you can be vulnerable? If so, how long did it take the relationship to develop?

    b. Describe the benefits of this friendship.

4. There are several trigger points that can turn a woman toward a cycle of fear. On your own, place a check next to each item with which you can personally identify.

☐ Lack of Trust
☐ Shyness
☐ Low Self-Esteem
☐ Shame
☐ Missed Opportunities
☐ Poor Communication Skills

Where are you on your journey to wholeness in these areas?

If you feel comfortable sharing one of your trigger points with the group, please do so. Everything shared in the group must remain confidential. Would you like the group to pray about this issue?

5. One way we try to cope with our fear of vulnerability is self-reliance. That's a form of sin. Another sinful coping mechanism is control or perfectionism. Behind these sinful strategies lies a false belief: God either isn't competent to care for us or doesn't value us enough to do so. In the following verses, what truths do you find that refute these false beliefs?
    Genesis 1:27

    Psalm 46:10

    Jeremiah 31:3

    2 Corinthians 12:9-10

    1 Peter 2:9

6. Dr. Paul Tournier once said, "No one can develop freely in this world and find a full life without feeling understood by at least one person. . . . [She] who would see [her]self clearly must open up to a confidant freely chosen and worthy of such trust."[5]

Do you agree or disagree with that statement? Explain.

7. The account of Jesus' life in the four Gospels gives us the answer to His remarkable power with people:

He looked at people, showing He really cared about them.
He touched people.

a. When have you experienced "kind eyes" and "appropriate touch" from someone?

b. What goes through your mind when you think about looking into the eyes of others and touching them appropriately as you build a friendship with them?

8. Read Philippians 1:29-30.
a. How does this passage show that Paul knew how to develop open, honest, and intimate friendships?

b. What personal application can you find for your own life?

9. What one thing will you do this week to be less controlling and more vulnerable with those closest to you?

WEEK 7

Read Chapter 7, "If I Don't Meet the Expectations of Others, What Will Happen to Them and Me?"

1. When you were growing up, who was the person you most wanted to please and *never* wanted to disappoint? Why did you feel that way?

2. Memorize Proverbs 29:25 (NIV). "Fear of man will prove to be a snare, but whoever trusts in the LORD is kept safe."

   a. Summarize that verse in your own words.

   b. In what specific ways has God "kept you safe" during the past month of your life?

3. If you are in a group, take turns reading through the following list of questions. As you read, put a mark in the box next to each question that you feel you should answer with yes.

   ☐ In one or more of your closest relationships, do you always give more than you receive?

   ☐ Do you fear arousing someone's anger or rage if you don't perform certain tasks to his or her liking?

   ☐ Do you "cover the tracks" for others you are close to by making excuses, justifying what they haven't done, doing work for them, or even lying to make them look better?

☐ Do you have trouble communicating in an open, honest, and appropriately confrontational manner with a certain person in your life?

☐ Do you find yourself "giving in" or "giving up" in order to keep peace in a relationship?

☐ Do the emotional mood swings of another person drastically affect your personal planning and emotional well-being?

☐ Do you find yourself constantly "fixing things" so someone else is in a good mood or behaves in a civil manner?

4. Select one of your yes responses and share any frustration you have regarding this issue with the group, without naming the person involved.

5. The fear of disappointing people is rooted in the fear of abandonment. Codependency can play a vital role in the lives of all of us who are afraid of disappointing people. Read Nancy Groom's definition of codependency and mutual interdependence on pages 116-117. On the scale that follows, indicate where you think you are in your most challenging personal relationship at this time in your life.

1	2	3	4	5	6	7	8	9	10
Debilitating Codependence								Healthy Mutual Interdependence	

6. Have you ever had the kind of interdependent relationship Groom describes? If so, what were the personal benefits you received?

7. When we face the fear of disappointing people or the fear of rejection, we often feel lonely. How does loneliness feel to you?

8. Summarize the truth you find in each of the following verses:
   Isaiah 54:10

   Ephesians 1:3-8

   Ephesians 3:17-19

   1 John 3:1

   What do these truths have to do with the fear of failing to meet others' expectations?

9. Look back at your summaries of the verses in question 8 and write a description of how God sees you.

10. If you are doing this study as a group, end the session with sentence prayers, thanking God for the specific things you've listed about His view of you. Example: "Thank you for adopting me into your family. . . . "

WEEK 8
Read Chapter 8, "What If the People I've Given My Love to Leave Me or Betray Me?"

1. If you were renewing a relationship with someone who once rejected you, which of the following scenarios would you prefer, and why?

   ☐ A very public gathering with many of your closest friends

☐ A long, quiet dinner with only the two of you

☐ A sporting event where the focus would be on *someone* or *something* other than your past issues with this person

☐ A brief encounter to test the waters

2. Memorize Hebrews 13:5-6 (NKJV): "For He Himself has said, 'I will never leave you nor forsake you.' So we may boldly say, 'The LORD is my helper; I will not fear. What can man do to me?'"

   a. If you have a small group, repeat the verse out loud together.

   b. Have you ever had someone walk away from you emotionally? If you feel comfortable telling how you responded and what you learned through that process, please share your experience with the group.

   c. How does the "mental adjustment" of knowing the Lord is your helper give you renewed confidence when you face rejection from someone you thought would "be there" for you?

3. The fear of rejection can be covered with subtle disguises. Place a check in the box next to any of the thoughts you have encountered when you considered developing a closer relationship with someone.

   ☐ If I tell you the truth about my past, you will push me away.

   ☐ If I'm vulnerable with you, I could be embarrassed.

   ☐ I have been betrayed by someone in the past, and it won't happen to me again.

☐ If I don't change my appearance, you will think I'm unattractive, and you might reject me.

☐ I feel threatened when you develop a close friendship with someone else.

☐ I feel unworthy of your love.

☐ I know you have many important things to do and many influential people in your life, so you probably don't really want to develop a friendship with someone like me.

☐ The people I've trusted the most in the past have let me down. I wonder when you will abandon me.

☐ I will work hard to avoid disappointing you, because if you reject me, I will have nobody.

4. Select one of the previous items. Describe how you worked through the fear and grew spiritually and personally as a result of this experience.

5. Read the intriguing story about Elijah recorded in 1 Kings 17.

   a. At what point in this chapter do you think Elijah felt abandoned?

   b. At what time in your life has your "brook dried up"?

   c. When you are abandoned — without the support of friends, family, or helpful resources — where do you turn?

6. Max Lucado says, "When all of earth turns against you, all of heaven turns toward you. To keep your balance in a crooked world, look at the mountains. Think of home."[6] Take a few minutes to list five things you can do today that will give you a "heavenly perspective"

in the middle of your current life situation. If you're meeting with a group, share your lists with each other.

7. There are four steps involved in a constructive choice to resolve the fear of being rejected.
   a. *Sorrow*. Read Job 19:17-20 and summarize the thoughts Job expressed during the time he felt abandoned.

   b. *Brokenness*. Read Psalm 51:1-5. Describe David's heart of confession to God.

   c. *Surrender.* Read Psalm 51:10-12. How did David show he was surrendering?

   d. *Faith-filled decision*. Review your memory verse, Hebrews 13:5-6. How can you come to a place of exchanging fear for faith on a daily basis?

8. What is the one thing you have learned so far during this study that will be helpful to you in the future? If you're meeting with a group, pair up with a partner to share your answers with each other and pray together.

WEEK 9

Read Chapter 9, "If I Remember and Reveal What Happened to Me, Will the Pain Be Insurmountable?"

1. When you have time to reflect, which of the following things are you the most likely to think about? Why do you think that's the case?

   ☐ Your mistakes of the past

   ☐ Your goals for the future

2. Memorize Psalm 103:10-12 (NIV). "He does not treat us as our sins deserve or repay us according to our iniquities. For as high as the heavens are above the earth, so great is his love for those who fear him; as far as the east is from the west, so far has he removed our transgressions from us."

   a. According to this verse, how does God treat us when we have messed up our lives and made wrong choices?

   b. What is the requirement for having our sins removed?

3. Read through the following list of "If onlys," and place a check in front of each one you can relate to.

   ☐ If only I could live that one day over . . .

   ☐ If only I had come to Christ sooner . . .

   ☐ If only I hadn't married the first man who showed an interest in me . . .

   ☐ If only I had taken the other route home . . .

   ☐ If only I could take back those words of criticism . . .

   ☐ If only I hadn't taken up that bad habit . . .

   ☐ If only I had left that miserable job sooner . . .

☐ If only I had resisted the flirtations of that man . . .

☐ If only I had spent more time with my children . . .

☐ If only I had the courage to confront my father/mother/ brother/grandfather about what (s)he did to me . . .

☐ If only I hadn't waited so long to have children . . .

4. As you look back on the "yesterdays" of your life, do you have any regret or painful memory that has been a hindrance to you? If you feel comfortable talking about it, share your thoughts with the group.

5. Many of us have been held in the grip of our fearful memories for too many years. Evaluate the way you currently feel about your past.

1	2	3	4	5	6	7	8	9	10

I am often consumed
with fears regarding
past issues.

I have resolved
my fears concerning
past issues.

6. Read through the following Scriptures and make any comment on God's instruction for dealing with the wrong choices of yesterday or His response to past issues.

Psalm 103:3-4

Psalm 103:10-12

1 Peter 5:6-7

1 John 1:9

7. Booker T. Washington once said, "I will not permit any man to narrow and degrade my soul by making me hate him."[7] I think Washington was really saying that when our days are consumed with thoughts of revenge, past abuses, or why we hate ourselves for the wrong choices we have made, we are chaining ourselves to a prison of our own making. How hard is it for you to forgive those who've wronged you and to forgive yourself for past mistakes? Explain.

8. Read Matthew 18:21-22. What do Jesus' words teach us about how God responds to our past mistakes when we ask for forgiveness?

9. Write down three words that describe what a forgiven woman feels like.

If you're meeting with a group, share your three words with them before closing in prayer.

WEEK 10

Read Chapter 10, "How Can I Have These Doubts About God and Call Myself a Christian?"

1. If you had serious doubts about your faith, who would you talk to? Why?

2. Memorize James 1:5-6 (NIV): "If any of you lacks wisdom, he should ask God, who gives generously to all without finding

fault, and it will be given to him. But when he asks, he must believe and not doubt, because he who doubts is like a wave of the sea, blown and tossed by the wind."

   a. Summarize the passage in your own words.

   b. James tells us we shouldn't doubt. How do you think a person with debilitating doubts gets past those doubts? Can she just decide, "Today I'm going to stop doubting"?

3. Read John 10:10.

   a. What expectations did you have when you became a Christian?

   b. How has your Christian experience been like or unlike what you expected?

4. Josh McDowell said, "For every confirmed skeptic I encounter, I meet at least a dozen sincere believers who struggle with doubt. At times their apprehension is casual, but at other times it is grave. These people want to believe God, but for whatever reason, wrestle with thoughts and feelings to the contrary. And, unfortunately, when doubt enters the believer's experience, it threatens to paralyze him."[8]

   Since you became a Christian, have you ever had serious doubts about the reality of God and/or His Word? If so, did you tell anybody about the struggle you were having, or was it too embarrassing to bring up?

5. Do you agree or disagree with the following statement? Explain. Doubts about God should not lead to denial, defeat, bitterness, or escape. They should lead to a "truth-search." Asking questions related to our doubts will lead to a strengthened faith as we discover truth in the process.

What advice do you have for the person (perhaps in your small group) who might be struggling with doubts about her faith right now?

6. Read Matthew 14:28-31.
    a. What was Jesus' question to Peter when he was struggling with fear?

    b. What do you think Peter's answer might have been? How do you think Jesus would have responded?

    c. What do you think Peter needed to do to get beyond fear and doubt to faith?

7. Have you ever had an experience in your life when you questioned whether or not there was a God, or whether a God of love could have allowed something bad to happen to you or to some-

one you love? Describe what happened and how you responded.

8. If you're meeting with a group, what thoughts and feelings do you have when someone describes a time of questioning?

9. Read 1 Peter 1:3-9. In your own words, explain Peter's description of an "eternal perspective" when bad things happen to good people.

10. If you're meeting with a group, close by praying honestly about your doubts and your desire for faith.

WEEK 11
Read Chapter 11, "What If I Never Live Up to My Potential?"

1. A cartoonist depicted a woman at a fork in the road who crashed into a pole between the two choices. As she stumbled out of her car with broken bones and open wounds, she said, "I just couldn't decide which way to go." Can you identify with this woman? Do you often find yourself paralyzed by indecision, or is it easy for you to make decisive choices?

2. Memorize Psalm 32:8 (NIV): "I will instruct you and teach you in the way you should go; I will counsel you and watch over you."
   a. What fear(s) does this verse help to eliminate?

b. What does the verse promise?

3. Many of us have been instructed to seek God's "perfect" plan for our lives, but sometimes that "plan" is elusive. Mark the box beside each of the following statements that you believe to be true.

☐ I believe God has a perfect blueprint for every Christian's life.
☐ I believe God gives Christians the right to choose regarding many life-altering options while still being in His will.
☐ I can be 100 percent sure of God's individual will for my life.
☐ I believe if a woman doesn't marry God's ideal man for her life, she will totally ruin the lives of the man she was supposed to marry and of the woman her husband was supposed to marry.

4. Read the following Scripture passages and summarize the truth you find.
   Psalm 19:7-8

   Proverbs 3:5-6

   Micah 6:8

5. Do you think these verses teach that there is a specific, inflexible blueprint for the believer, or that God's will might involve wider choices, within His guidelines, for a successful and meaningful Christian life? Explain.

6. Some of the fears of getting trapped in a dead-end life situation are hard to eliminate.

   a. Place a mark in the box next to each fear that is similar to one you have experienced.

   ☐ If I can't get away from the ugliness of my past, I will be destined for failure.

   ☐ If I take *this* job now because of economic necessity, I may close the door on a better opportunity for career advancement in a position more suited to my background and education.

   ☐ If I don't work harder and outdo the competition in my office, I may not get a promotion.

   ☐ If I'm promoted, I may feel pressured to "succeed" at a level that will compromise balance in other important areas of my life.

   ☐ If I say no to personal or professional opportunities in order to stay physically and emotionally healthy now, I may never have other opportunities when I'm ready for them.

   ☐ If I choose to marry, I may get a man as dysfunctional as my father, and I will never let that happen!

   ☐ If I don't marry *this* man, someone I'm more compatible with might not come along, and I'd be sorry I turned him down.

   ☐ If I have a baby now, I may interrupt my career and never recapture the momentum and job success I've worked so hard to obtain.

   ☐ If I wait to have a child until I'm older and more established in my marriage and in my career, I may not be able to get pregnant.

   ☐ If I don't pursue infertility treatment, I will never know complete fulfillment as a mother and eventually as a grandmother.

b. Which of the previous scenarios has brought you the greatest fear of getting trapped?

c. What escapes, if any, are you using right now to numb the fear of failure in your life?

d. What is the most tangible thing you could offer to God right now that would represent your surrender to Him?

7. Read the story of Janet on pages 184-188. What is the main lesson you learn from her example? How will it influence your future choices?

8. Pray (with your group or on your own), "Lord, help us to base our daily choices on our knowledge of Your character and Your Word. Give us the wisdom to seek wise counsel by talking to You first and by talking to godly people who walk closely with You."

WEEK 12
Read Chapter 12, "What If Reaching My Goals Isn't Enough?"

1. In what one area of your life are you the most afraid of failing?

2. Memorize Isaiah 41:10 (NIV): "So do not fear, for I am with you; do

not be dismayed, for I am your God. I will strengthen you and help you; I will uphold you with my righteous right hand."

   a. In what area of your life do you most need God to calm your fears and give you strength right now?

   b. Speak this verse aloud in unison, if you are doing this study in a small group. Later, share the verse through e-mail or in an encouragement telephone call to someone who isn't in the class.

3. What has God been speaking to your heart during the twelve sessions of this study?

4. What part of the constructive resolution for dealing with fear is the greatest challenge for you? Explain.

   ☐ *Sorrow*: Allowing yourself to grieve over fear brought on by a fallen world.
   ☐ *Brokenness*: Experiencing true humility before God with your focus off the fear and on Him.
   ☐ *Surrender*: Giving up your self-reliance by a specific act of "heart submission" and choosing God-dependence.
   ☐ *Faith-filled decisions*: The ability to choose faith over fear in real-life situations.

5. H. Norman Wright says, "You have failed in the past. You are failing now in some way. You will fail in the future. You weren't perfect in the past. You won't be perfect in the future. Your children
   will not be perfect, either. When you fail, allow yourself to feel
   disappointment, but not disapproval. . . . You can fail and not be a
   failure!"[9]

   a. Do you agree or disagree with H. Norman Wright that you
      can fail and not be a failure? Explain.

   b. What is failure's potentially positive contribution to your
      life? (Check page 204 for some ideas, if needed.)

6. Read Philippians 3:13-14. What was Paul's secret that enabled
   him to look at the future without fear and regret? How would you
   explain it in your own words?

7. Which chapter of *Tame Your Fears* was the most meaningful to
   you personally? Why?

8. If you're meeting with a group, how can the group pray for you
   specifically?

After praying for these needs, close the study by praying aloud the following prayer:

Lord, give me the grace to realize life on this earth will never be completely free from anxiety. I know the enemy will harass me with fear for the future and with memories of past failures. I will be tempted to fall back into old patterns of handling my fears.

Protect me from the bondage of denial and defeat. Guard my heart from the cancer of bitterness. Keep me from my favorite escapes into perfectionism and workaholism.

Lord, when fear surfaces, help me to grieve over the pain without shame and let my broken heart turn me to humble surrender and forgiveness. Enable me to practice making faith-filled decisions as I submit to Your authority in my life. Keep me from demanding instant answers and help me to understand the simple truth: Faith that begins with fear will end up closer to You. Amen.

NOTES

CHAPTER ONE

"If I'm Such a Great Christian, Why Do I Have This Problem?"
1. *Webster's New World Dictionary of the American Language*, s.v. "fear."
2. *Webster's New World Dictionary.*
3. Peter McWilliams, "Happiness . . . Understanding Happiness," *Bottom Line* 14, no.1 (15 January 1993): p. 1.
4. Henri J. M. Nouwen, "Prayer and the Jealous God," *New Oxford Review* 52 (June 1985): pp. 9-10. Used by permission.
5. Paraphrased from 1 John 4:18.

CHAPTER TWO

"What Happens Inside My Head When I'm Afraid?"
1. Paul Moede, "Facing Down the Giants in Your Land," *Discipleship Journal,* no. 52 (1989): p. 24.
2. Paraphrased from Matthew 14:22-33.
3. Paraphrased from many books and dictionaries.

CHAPTER THREE

"Why Do I Let Irrational Panic Immobilize Me?"
1. Marcia J. Pear, "How to Turn Off the Anxiety Alarm," quoted from *Nation's Business,* August 1992, p. 60. Copyright 1992, U.S. Chamber of Commerce.
2. Pear, p. 60.
3. Jacqueline Wasser, "Phobias, Panic, and Fear—Oh My!" *Mademoiselle* 96, April 1990, p. 162.
4. Carl Bard, quoted by Barbara Johnson, *Pack Up Your Gloomies in a Great Big Box* (Dallas, Tex.: Word, 1993), p. 26.
5. Lawrence Richards, *Lawrence Richards' 365 Day Devotional Commentary* (Wheaton, Ill.: Victor, 1990), p. 342.

6. *Webster's New World Dictionary of the American Language.*

7. Amanda Warren, "Scare Tactics —Living With Your Secret Fears," *Mademoiselle,* October 1991, p. 98.

8. Nicky Marone, *Women and Risk: How to Master Your Fears and Do What You Never Thought You Could Do* (New York: St. Martin's Press, 1992), p. xi (preface).

9. This account is found in Exodus 3:11-12; 4:1-13 (NIV).

CHAPTER FOUR

"Why Does the Fear of Things That Might Happen Consume My Mental and Spiritual Energy?"
1. Karen Randau, *Conquering Fear* (Houston and Dallas, Tex.: Rapha Publishing/Word, 1991), p. 5.

2. Randau, p. 5.

3. Jane and Robert Handly with Pauline Neff, "Why Can't I Stop Worrying?" *Ladies' Home Journal,* January 1991, p. 88.

4. Sharlene King, "How to Feel Better About the Future," *Ladies' Home Journal,* May 1992, p. 94.

5. King, p. 94.

6. Barbara Johnson, *Stick a Geranium in Your Hat and Be Happy* (Dallas, Tex.: Word, 1990), pp. 72-73.

7. Nicky Marone, *Women and Risk: How to Master Your Fears and Do What You Never Thought You Could Do* (New York: St. Martin's Press, 1992), p. 17.

8. Marone, p. 17.

9. Handly and Neff, p. 88.

10. This incident is found in Luke 1:28-38.

11. Sue Monk Kidd, *When the Heart Waits* (San Francisco, Calif.: Harper & Row, 1990), p. 114.

12. Barbara Johnson, *Splashes of Joy in the Cesspools of Life* (Dallas, Tex: Word, 1992), p. 101.

CHAPTER FIVE

"Why Does Everything I Do Have to Be Perfect?"
1. Barbara Sullivan, *The Control Trap* (Minneapolis, Minn.: Bethany House, 1991), p. 73.

2. *New Webster's Dictionary and Thesaurus of the English Language,* s.v. "vulnerable."

3. Paula Rinehart, *Perfect Every Time* (Colorado Springs, Colo.: NavPress, 1992), p. 18-19.
4. Chris Thurman, "Perfectionism," *Today's Better Life,* Spring 1993, p. 48.
5. Rinehart, p. 25.
6. Les Carter, *Imperative People* (Nashville, Tenn.: Nelson, 1991), p. 47.
7. Found in Psalm 51:1-10.

CHAPTER SIX

"If I Let You Get Close to Me, Will You Still Like Me?"

1. Dr. Paul Tournier, as quoted in John Powell, S.J., *Why Am I Afraid to Tell You Who I Am?* (Allen, Tex: Tabor Publishing, 1969), p. 20.
2. Susan Jacoby, "The Guarded Girl: What Is She Hiding?" *Cosmopolitan,* October 1992, p. 231.
3. Jacoby, p. 231.
4. Max Lucado, *Six Hours One Friday* (Portland, Ore.: Multnomah, 1989), p. 36.
5. David Seamands, *Healing of Memories* (Wheaton, Ill.: Victor, 1985), p. 84.
6. Powell, p. 52.
7. Powell, pp. 54-61. (The five levels of communication were first introduced in this way by John Powell.)
8. Powell, p. 61.
9. Jacoby, p. 232.

CHAPTER SEVEN

"If I Don't Meet the Expectations of Others, What Will Happen to Them and Me?"

1. Although this is an accurate portrayal of my sister's story, names and identifying details have been changed to protect the privacy of people involved.
2. Curt Grayson and Jan Johnson, *Creating a Safe Place* (New York: HarperCollins, 1991), p. 23.
3. Nancy Groom, *From Bondage to Bonding* (Colorado Springs, Colo.: NavPress, 1991), p. 21.
4. Groom, p. 21.
5. Katherine Ketcham and Ginny Lyford Gustafson, *Living on the Edge* (New York: Bantam Books, 1989), p. 77.

6. Robert Hemfelt, Frank Minirth, and Paul Meier, *Love Is a Choice* (Nashville, Tenn.: Thomas Nelson, 1989), pp. 98-99.

7. Hemfelt, Minirth, and Meier, p. 99.

Chapter Eight

"What If the People I've Given My Love to Leave Me or Betray Me?"

1. Lloyd Ogilvie, *12 Steps to Living Without Fear* (Waco, Tex.: Word, 1987), p. 111.

2. Margery D. Rosen, "All Alone: The New Loneliness of American Women," *Ladies Home Journal*, April 1991, p. 218.

3. Rosen, p. 218.

4. Max Lucado, *And the Angels Were Silent* (Portland, Ore.: Multnomah, 1992), p. 159.

5. Ogilvie, p. 128.

6. Calvin Miller, "Alone," *Moody*, March 1991, pp. 22-23.

Chapter Nine

"If I Remember and Reveal What Happened to Me, Will the Pain Be Insurmountable?"

1. Larry Crabb, *Inside Out* (Colorado Springs, Colo.: NavPress, 1988), p. 120.

2. Alfred Ells, *Restoring Innocence* (Nashville, Tenn.: Thomas Nelson, 1990), p. 51.

3. Paraphrase from Dan B. Allender, *The Wounded Heart* (Colorado Springs, Colo.: NavPress, 1992), p. 57.

4. C. S. Lewis, *The Problem of Pain* (New York: Macmillan, 1978), p. 93.

5. David B. Biebel, *If God Is So Good, Why Do I Hurt So Bad?* (Colorado Springs, Colo.: NavPress, 1989), p. 128.

6. Booker T. Washington, as quoted in *Great Quotes & Illustrations*, compiled by George Sweeting (Waco, Tex.: Word, 1985), p. 119.

7. Judith Sills, Ph.D., *Excess Baggage* (New York: Viking Penguin, 1993), pp. 229-230.

Chapter Ten

"How Can I Have These Doubts About God and Call Myself a Christian?"

1. Jackie Hudson, *Doubt, A Road to Growth* (San Bernardino, Calif.: Here's Life, 1987), p. 13.

2. Hudson, p. 14.
3. Hudson, p. 14.
4. Ken Abraham, *The Disillusioned Christian* (San Bernardino, Calif.: Here's Life, 1991), p. 11.
5. Paula Rinehart, "Passages of Faith," *Discipleship Journal,* May/June 1993, p. 19.
6. Rinehart, p. 19.
7. Gary Parker, *The Gift of Doubt: From Crisis to Authentic Faith* (San Francisco, Calif.: Harper & Row, 1990), pp. 142-143.

CHAPTER ELEVEN

"What If I Never Live Up to My Potential?"
1. J. I. Packer, *Knowing God* (Downers Grove, Ill.: InterVarsity, 1973), p. 30.
2. Garry Friesen, *Decision Making and the Will of God* (Portland, Ore.: Multnomah, 1980), book jacket.
3. Haddon W. Robinson, quoted in the foreword of Friesen, p. 13.
4. Dr. Arthur Freeman and Rose DeWolf, *Woulda, Coulda, Shoulda* (New York: HarperPerennial, 1990), p. 23.
5. Curt Grayson and Jan Johnson, *Creating a Safe Place* (New York: Harper San Francisco, 1991), p. 118.
6. Edward Kuhlman, *An Overwhelming Interference* (Old Tappan, N.J.: Revell, 1986), p. 18.
7. Barbara Johnson, *Pack Up Your Gloomies in a Great Big Box* (Dallas, Tex: Word, 1993), p. 66.
8. Paraphrased from Friesen, p. 92.
9. Mary Lou Cummings, quoted in *Inspiring Quotations,* compiled by Albert M. Wells, Jr. (Nashville, Tenn.: Thomas Nelson, 1988), p. 56.
10. Gordon Graham, quoted in *Quotable Quotations,* compiled by Lloyd Cory (Wheaton, Ill.: Victor, 1985), p. 96.
11. Elizabeth Dole, quoted from a speech given at the National Prayer Breakfast, 5 February 1987.

CHAPTER TWELVE

"What If Reaching My Goals Isn't Enough?"
1. Carol Kent, *Speak Up With Confidence* (Nashville, Tenn.: Thomas Nelson, 1987), p. 172.
2. Erwin Lutzer, *Quotable Quotes,* complied by Lloyd Cory (Wheaton, Ill.: Victor, 1985), p. 371.

3. Helen Keller, quoted in *Leadership* 13, no. 3 (Summer 1992): p. 30.
4. David Frahm, *The Great Niche Hunt* (Colorado Springs, Colo.: NavPress, 1991), pp. 144-145.
5. H. Norman Wright, quoted by Judy Anderson, "Learning Unconditional Love," *Moody,* February 1993, p. 53.
6. Bruce Larson, *Living Beyond Our Fears* (New York: Harper San Francisco, 1990), p. 150.

Twelve-Week Bible Study

1. John-Roger and Peter McWilliams, *The Portable DO IT!* (Los Angeles, Calif.: Prelude Press, 1992), p. 42.
2. Corrie ten Boom, quoted in *Quotable Quotations,* compiled by Lloyd Cory (Wheaton, Ill.: Victor, 1985), pp. 446-447.
3. Barbara Sullivan, *The Control Trap* (Minneapolis, Minn.: Bethany House, 1991), p. 37.
4. *New Webster's Dictionary and Thesaurus of the English Language,* s.v. "vulnerable."
5. Dr. Paul Tournier, as quoted in John Powell, S.J., *Why Am I Afraid to Tell You Who I Am?* (Allen, Tex.: Tabor Publishing, 1969), p. 5.
6. Max Lucado, *And the Angels Were Silent* (Portland, Ore.: Multnomah, 1992), p. 163.
7. Booker T. Washington, quoted in *Great Quotes & Illustrations,* compiled by George Sweeting (Waco, Tex.: Word, 1985), p. 119.
8. Josh McDowell, quoted in the foreword of *Doubt, A Road to Growth,* by Jackie Hudson (San Bernadino, Calif.: Here's Life, 1987), p. 9.
9. H. Norman Wright, quoted by Judy Anderson, "Learning Unconditional Love," *Moody,* February 1993, p. 53.

AUTHOR

CAROL KENT is the president of Speak Up Speaker Services, a Christian speakers' bureau, and the founder and director of Speak Up With Confidence seminars, a ministry committed to helping Christians develop their communication skills.

A member of the National Speakers Association, Carol is a nationally known speaker for conferences and retreats throughout the United States and Canada. A former radio show cohost, Carol has a B.S. degree in speech education and an M.A. in communication arts from Western Michigan University. She has been a featured speaker on "Focus on the Family" radio broadcasts and at the Praise Gathering for Believers. She has also been a keynoter for the Heritage Keepers and Time Out for Women arena events. She is a popular guest on a wide variety of radio and television programs and has been featured in a cover interview in *Today's Christian Woman* magazine.

Her books include *Becoming a Woman of Influence, Tame Your Fears, Speak Up With Confidence, Mothers Have Angel Wings,* and *Detours, Tow Trucks, and Angels in Disguise.* She has also co-written the *Designed for Influence Bible Study Series* with Karen Lee-Thorp, along with the guided journal, *My Soul's Journey: Becoming Who God Wants Me To Be* (all NavPress)

Carol and her husband, Gene, make their home in Port Huron, Michigan. They have one grown son and two granddaughters.

To schedule Carol Kent to speak for your next event, please contact
Speak Up Speaker Services toll free at (888) 870-7719
or by e-mail at: Speakupinc@aol.com
www.SpeakUpSpeakerServices.com

Rock solid advice for tumultuous times.

Becoming a Woman of Influence

If you want your life to count for eternity, this book will help you learn to have a lasting, godly impact on other people's lives.

(Carol Kent)

Calm My Anxious Heart

If you feel like worry is ruling your life or you only trust God when things go right, this twelve-week study will help you focus on growing in contentment and faith as you learn to trust God completely. Companion journal also available.

(Linda Dillow)

Under the Circumstances

Discover how a change in perspective can help you learn to live above the circumstances.

(Judy Hampton)

Choosing Rest

Author Sally Breedlove shows us how to choose God's perfect gift of rest, even in the midst of our restless lives.

(Sally Breedlove)

To get your copies, visit your local bookstore, call 1-800-366-7788, or log on to www.navpress.com. Ask for a FREE catalog of NavPress products. Offer #BPA.

NAVPRESS

BRINGING TRUTH TO LIFE
www.navpress.com